URGENCY ADDICTION

URGENCY ADDICTION

HOW TO SLOW DOWN
WITHOUT SACRIFICING SUCCESS

Nina Tassi, Ph.D.

TAYLOR PUBLISHING COMPANY
DALLAS, TEXAS

For Al With Love

Published by Taylor Publishing Company
         1550 West Mockingbird Lane
         Dallas, Texas 75235

Designed by Hespenheide Design

Library of Congress Cataloging-in-Publication Data
Tassi, Nina.
    Urgency addiction : how to slow down without sacrificing success /
Nina Tassi.
        p.   cm.
    ISBN 0-87833-732-6 : $18.95
    1. Time—Psychological aspects.   2. Work—Psychological aspects.
3. Success in business—United States—Psychological aspects.
4. Success—United States—Psychological aspects.   5. National
characteristics, American.   I. Title.
    BF637.T5T37   1991
    640′.43—dc20   90-21581
                                                                        CIP

Printed in the United States of America

10 9 8 7 6 5 4 3 2 1

Contents

Preface

Picture this. A scorching orange sun beats down on a young man sprinting up Wall Street in New York City. Dressed and groomed to perfection in standard business costume, he clutches in one hand an expensive briefcase made of the carbon fiber space travelers use, while he raises his free hand to stare frantically at his large gold Rolex. The unusual feature about this businessman is the pair of glittering wax-and-feather wings that jut out from his shoulder blades and appear to be attached to his suit. As he runs, he glances back at these wings, terrified that the sun will burn them up and utterly destroy him before he gets to his next appointment.

This man is mythic. But in America today millions like him pursue their careers as descendants of an ancient figure described by the poet Ovid. As the tale goes, the exiled Daedalus was imprisoned on the island of Crete. Yearning for home, he created an escape device: two pairs of gold wax-and-feather wings—for himself and his son Icarus. When he attached the wings to his son, Daedalus warned the youth not to fly too high or too low, but to steer a middle course. Once in the sky, however, Icarus became enchanted by the pleasures of flight, soaring faster and higher until he approached the blazing sun. His wings burst into flame, and he plunged down to the sea and destruction.

This book is about our condition as modern Icaruses: how it came about for many Americans that we got seduced into flying so fast and so high that we stay in peril of losing our very selves. This is a book not about a personality problem, but about a cultural phenomenon: how time took us over in the late twentieth century. Most important, it is also about how to overcome the time distortion which has invaded us. From this book you will learn how to achieve a new and balanced sense of time.

You may be a present-day Icarus. You may work every day at a demon pace, but find your tracks haunted by the specter of time. Or it could be that the exorbitant demands on your time force you to hurry everywhere, whether at home or at the office. Maybe it is simply that you never have a minute to yourself.

This sense of time urgency is what I call Urgency Addiction—an invisible but real feeling of constant time pressure. Although this phenomenon pervades our American culture, it has not been fully recognized and described until now. The inner sense of time which we carry with us through life normally goes unnoticed. We go through our days not paying attention directly to the invisible reality of time—until something goes wrong.

Time has gone awry for many Americans. A society of speed-worshippers, we are living at a pace of ever-accelerating change. Speed—whether for its own sake or because we believe faster is inevitably better—is our ruling standard. We run a treadmill constantly getting notched up to a slightly faster pace, and we are made to feel that our task is to keep up—at any cost. Running so hard, we haven't noticed that our perception has been distorted.

Most of us have felt enormous increases in the demands on our time: new mothers returning to work six weeks after childbirth who need suitable day care in a hurry; fathers who must spend longer stretches at the office just to keep their jobs in workplaces teeming with rumors of corporate takeovers and buyouts; young professionals new to the workforce who find that the fast track mandates 60-hour weeks; and, beyond the work environment, a society where the communications media, from advertising to entertainment, all scream for our instant attention.

These are everyday realities for millions of Americans. Meanwhile, the traditional family supports that once eased the pressures of time have largely disappeared. Where is the nearby grandma to care for the baby? Where is the stay-at-home mother whose husband is out earning the bread? Where are the aunt, uncle, and cousin to call in times of sickness and troubles? They're either at work or living in another part of the country.

Now, many thousands of single working parents have no family members to call on for help. The nuclear family has been replaced by the blended family in which complex stepparent/stepchildren relationships require tremendous outputs of time and emotional energy. Beyond that are untold thousands of young singles putting in incredibly long hours of work and—in their after-hours—trying to find a community of friends, often in a city where no family members live. This new social reality adds another layer of time pressure.

Is it possible to get free of this feeling? This book answers yes. You can get free, moreover, without sacrificing career success or anything else that matters in your life. You can transform time from a tyrant into an ally and friend.

This book is the result of a personal journey I made after finding myself caught in the time trap a few years ago. This feeling of having Time's wingèd chariot always at my back—to paraphrase Andrew Marvell's lines—began almost without my noticing that it was interfering with my life. It crept up on me, gradually taking away most of my daily pleasures and eventually a large part of my happiness. My search for the solution to this awful burden of time pressure took me—in imagination—around the globe. I suspected almost from the start that my sense of time urgency had its roots not in my personality (since I hadn't always felt this terrible pressure), but somewhere in the broader American culture. I was soon drawn farther afield to the world as a whole. The forces at work on me were revealed as stronger and deeper—in time and space—than I had imagined at the beginning of my journey.

My search led me to interview people from many walks of life, and to study books by experts in economics and sociology, philosophy and business. I sought out successful people who struck me as possessing the secret of *time-integration*, which is the term I coined to describe that attractive and instantly recognizable quality in the busy, successful person who gives you complete attention as you talk, never seems hurried, and exudes an aura of contentment and self-possession. It's a quality which makes you desire to be with that person, to be like him or her. I came to recognize this quality as one I used to have but had somehow lost. I wanted to get it back.

My purpose was practical. I wanted to find out why I—and so many others—experienced this sense of time urgency, in order to discover how to get free of it. I knew it had to be something deeper than the usual time management advice: I was already super-organized and a devotee of such time gurus as Alan Lakein, author of *How To Get Control of Your Time and Your Life.*

What is the "right" sense of time? I wondered. Is there such a thing as a "natural pace" or a "natural flow" of time? Do they change with the "seasons," the varying circumstances of a person's life? The one thing I felt sure of was that it wasn't good to feel constantly harried by time. Was there a way out of the dilemma?

The answers I found make up this book. I am convinced it will help you, and bring you pleasures you may have forgotten or perhaps never knew. It will show you how time can be the source of self-renewal, creativity, and greater success in your career.

During my research, many people with time urgency confided to me that they feel a vague sense of bereavement. Something necessary and precious has disappeared—the experience of that natural ease and rhythm of time flowing through their days. They run through their days feeling harried and hurried. They experience a chipping away at their sense of well-being and self-esteem.

Early in my search, as I began to interview friends, relatives, colleagues—some of whom I was on quite intimate terms with—I found to my surprise, over and over again, that when I began probing them about their time, a strange reticence, even embarrassment, would come over them. Unintentionally, I had stepped into very private territory. I began to see that time is our most intimate possession. In a very real and strange way, my time is my self.

My goal is to help you free yourself from the distress of time pressure. I understand that the heart of the problem for most people with time urgency is the job. That is why I have devoted the entire last section of the book, Taking Back Ownership of Your Work Time, to solving the problem of time pressure on the job. I know, because I've already encountered it many times in my interviews, that your first response will be: "Nothing can be done. My job demands that I put in these hours. I'll lose my job if I try to get away from time pressure." What I want to show you is that, at best, you're paying too high a price for success, and at worst, you are actually setting yourself up for failure in the 1990s. As corporations keep getting leaner and meaner in order to succeed in the new era of global competition, the simple expedient of putting in atrociously long hours for the company will not save your head from the chopping block.

This is not another book about time management. New times require new solutions. This book will teach you not simply how to cope with time pressure but how to cure it. You can achieve mastery over the time of your life.

Finally, this is a book about the American Dream and how to achieve it in your life. Returning home after traversing the globe, I bring this message: Your time belongs to you. Let me show you how to get it back.

Understanding
Urgency Addiction

1
PEOPLE CAUGHT IN TIME TRAPS

But at my back I always hear

Time's wingèd chariot hurrying near.

—ANDREW MARVELL, "TO HIS COY MISTRESS"

Ours was a storybook romance. After a dozen years of marriage we were still deeply in love. But one morning my husband and I woke up and turned to each other in shock. What we saw mirrored in each other's eyes horrified us.

Everybody we knew thought we had it all—vigorous health and good looks, a marriage like the Rock of Gibraltar, three terrific kids, successful careers. We thought so too. But on that unforgettable morning everything changed. My husband wore an expression close to despair. Afterwards he said that my face looked as if I had just run screaming out of a haunted house.

We had no time to talk. Every second counted. We had to hit the floor running, with ourselves and three children to get showered, dressed, fed, schoolbags and lunch boxes packed, maybe a last-minute homework check, then carpooling duties for half the neighborhood, and finally, on to our respective jobs—all accomplished at breakneck speed. Our next free time together would be around midnight, when we agreed to meet.

Nearly seventeen hours later we tumbled into bed, exhausted, then lay with pillows propped up talking until dawn. Neither of us could give a name to the problem that had appeared out of the blue, but we realized that whatever "it" was, all the fun had gone out of our lives.

"It's worse than that," I murmured. "I feel pressured all the time. It's like being on a merry-go-round that keeps whirling faster and faster until it makes me so dizzy I can't jump off." Bursting into tears, I proceeded to cry my eyes out. His arms around me, my husband confessed that he, too, felt harried by our schedules—as he put it, "the relentless round of chores, the endless worry about logistics." It seemed a trivial cause of distress so severe.

3

We were caught in the time trap, although at the time we didn't know what it was or how to escape from it. But that all-night meeting in bed marked the starting point for this book. I began a journey then in search of answers, determined to go on until I discovered and understood the hurrying disease which I have named Urgency Addiction—a name needed because until now it has gone unrecognized as the powerful phenomenon which it surely is. Along the way, I interviewed many people—college students, mothers and fathers, lawyers, physicians, corporate executives—who suffered from time pressures even more intensely than my husband and I did. Some of those I encountered were so addicted to the clock that they had lost touch with their identities.

The search was fruitful. I discovered a way to climb out of the time trap. This is the story of the people who gave me the clues to find a path back to freedom. Let me begin by describing the daily lives of three people, whom I've given the pseudonyms of Melissa, Stephanie, and Wayne. They shared with me the intimate details of their experiences and feelings in an effort to help paint a true picture of time distortion in America. Their stories reveal the significant shapes that time pressure takes when it invades our lives as successful Americans.

Melissa: A Lawyer at the Mercy of Billable Hours

Melissa is a 28-year-old lawyer on the fast track. A gorgeous woman with glistening long black hair, she favors gray Armani suits and silk shirts as she pursues a rigorous daily schedule. Each morning she artfully conceals with makeup the dark circles under her eyes from lack of sleep and manages to reach her office before 7:45 A.M.

The prestigious law firm where she works takes up all the suites on the thirtieth floor and opens onto an elegant reception parlor furnished in old-money taste with Oriental carpets, carved-oak panelling, an antique highboy against one wall. Behind double oak doors runs a long corridor punctuated by associates' offices. Melissa is pleased when she finds the hall dimly lit: a sign of being the first arrival. She hurries straight to her office.

Melissa kicks off her Reeboks, replacing them with stylish Bruno Maglis, and glances at the clock (a deeply ingrained habit frequently resorted to) as she pulls from her briefcase a stack of folders which she worked on at home the night before. Before getting started, she takes a hairbrush and gives her hair a few vigorous strokes. Melissa's hair, reaching halfway down her back, marks her one statement of independence, she explained to me on our first interview. Back at Harvard, when her friends heard she'd landed a spot with this noted law firm, they said she would never get away with that hair. Melissa had simply laughed, determined to make it her way—and fast.

Four years later, she flaunts her long hair but seldom laughs. The stakes are too high and the moment of reckoning too close. Every day is meticulously planned down to the minute, each agenda item reading "partner" in invisible letters to reinforce her goal: to make partner before age 30.

The firm doesn't require attendance at the weekly associates' meeting, but rarely does a young attorney miss the chance to score points against a colleague. Melissa always walks in keyed up, ready for battle. Coffee poured, she joins a dozen people at the polished mahogany conference table. Tom ambles in, *The Wall Street Journal* tucked under his arm, at 8:00 sharp. This demigod, the senior partner and great-grandson of the founder, displays the demeanor of a Southern gentleman as he waxes eloquent about the firm's illustrious tradition.

"But I was never fooled," says Melissa. His heavy body sinking into a leather chair, his pudgy manicured hand fluttering her way: such lazy gestures mask a razor-sharp brain that does multimillion-dollar deals with ease. From day one she knew that her fate hung on the flicker of an eyelid from him. Unless she pleased him, she wouldn't make junior partner.

Being a Token Isn't Enough

Melissa follows the same ritual every meeting, surveying her competitors: two Stanfords, one Columbia, an NYU who got in because his uncle is a senior partner, a Yalie ("What a snot!" she always thinks when she runs through this ritual), and two other Harvards (both *Law Review* editors) besides herself. She perceived early on that her gender gives her leverage in this conservative firm. They're modernizing their image discreetly to attract new money; employing a few female lawyers helps. Melissa also knows, however, that being a token isn't enough—not by a long shot.

At every meeting Melissa notes a trickle of sweat at the small of her back, unpreventable even after four years of consistently brilliant performance. "I would die before I'd let anybody know I felt nervous," she confided to me once. "Never let them see the chink in the armor." As soon as a colleague presents a case, Melissa launches into her critique. Tom leans back with a Cheshire grin to enjoy the fight. Points will be won or lost here in the competition to make partner. The contenders are many, but few will be chosen.

Tom often reminds them that they work for a magnanimous firm: they're not required to keep corporate hours, and may come and go as they please.

There is one catch. Each attorney must bill clients for a total of 1,700 hours per year. That means constant pressure to attract new clients (or find more work with current clients) in order to pile up the necessary billed hours. That translates into many more hours per week than the theoretical 40.

"When I first joined the firm," Melissa explained, "I felt unbelievably free." After seven years on the academic treadmill, her eye on the clock night and day, aiming for a perfect record, she thought she'd finally escaped. Not that it hadn't been worth it: she graduated *summa cum laude* and Phi Beta Kappa from Columbia, then plucked the juicy plum of Harvard Law School.

Before starting law school she had wanted to take a year off. Her fantasy: to hitchhike out West, bum around in blue jeans for a few months, get some sunshine, breathe fresh air, maybe learn mountain climbing. But her dad talked her out of it. Didn't she want the fast track? Her mother, also a lawyer, agreed. Taking time off was out of the quer on. When she finished law school would be a better time.

But that also proved impossible. Too many super-bright women were flooding the field. She could lose her edge as a female lawyer. So she forged ahead. With a straight-A record from Harvard, except for one B+ she managed to explain away, Melissa got her reward—a starting salary of $80,000, plus some of the best legal minds in the country for colleagues.

Sixty-Hour Weeks

It was heady. Better than men, which she never had time for, anyway. But the freedom soon dissipated. Those billable hours never added up fast enough. By the time she'd been with the firm six months, Melissa routinely put in 60-hour weeks. As she told me, "An easy day is 9 to 7." In a hectic week, she puts in 70 hours. She has stopped separating work hours from personal time.

Most of her colleagues go bar-hopping on Saturday nights, drinking till dawn, and many of them take cocaine, but she avoids that scene. Making it in her career is too important. Melissa works out with a personal trainer at a nearby gym three times a week from 6 to 7 A.M., determined to keep in top form until she makes partner. Then she plans to take time off.

If the meeting in-house drags, somewhere around 9:20 A.M. Melissa feels a familiar knot tie up her stomach as she mentally rearranges her day, shaving off minutes here and there to make up for the losses. Everyone bolts for the offices the instant Tom waves them away. Melissa runs through her phone messages, makes some quick calls, and darts out to hail a cab. Once inside the taxi, she checks her watch for the dozenth time of the morning and takes a deep breath, instructs her taut muscles to relax. Two hours after she gets them loosened up in the gym, they've snapped as tight as a cobra's jaw.

A woman who prides herself on self-control, Melissa told me about a recent incident that troubled her. As her taxi lurched past her turn on Lexington Avenue, she yelled at the cabbie. "Hey! Where do you think you're going?" She couldn't believe how angry her voice sounded, and when the cabbie snarled back, she felt a surge of tears. Horrified, she clapped a hand over her mouth, afraid of releasing an uncontrollable flood. She also described a recurring nightmare in which she holds a mirror up to her face and sees that she's turned gray overnight—all her beautiful black hair has become an ugly steel-gray.

Often these days Melissa calms herself with a ritual she traces back to childhood. She counts the months, then weeks, then days until she comes up for partner. The pressure will end, and she can take some time for herself. She never considers the possibility of not making partner. She's worked incredible hours, postponed most pleasures, never wasted a minute. She owes it to herself to make it before she reaches 30.

She maintains perfect composure with clients. On the elevator she reviews a client's case, and by the time she is ushered into the office, the adrenaline is pumping hard. Gone is the sense of time urgency that stalks her days, the memory of the nights when she pops awake, drenched in sweat, heart pounding from a nightmare. Practicing law, her performance is splendid. After an appointment Melissa characteristically walks on air to the next appointment. Recently she experienced perfection. At the conclusion of an excellent meeting, her best client supplied (unsolicited) two names of prospective new clients. The billable hours problem instantly receded into the background. Melissa could see herself clocking plenty of billable hours without having to go out and hustle new clients for a while.

Melissa's days flash by. She often stays late at the office, sending out for Chinese food and working until 10 P.M., sometimes 10:30.

Long, Hard Nights

By the time she gets back to her apartment, the weariness seeps through her muscles so that sometimes she feels she can hardly stand up. Often she suppresses an urge to drink a quart of milk and eat a whole box of cookies; staying thin is essential to her power image.

Nights are hard. Melissa undresses and goes into the bathroom where, looking in the mirror, she is startled at how much darker her circles have gotten since morning and at how strongly she resembles her mother. Time speeds up. She feels she's turning old before her very eyes.

Once in bed, Melissa thinks about her mother, a senior partner in a reputable Baltimore firm. Why does she work so many hours, Melissa wonders, when there is no need? She is known throughout the state as a spokesperson for many causes; she has argued before the Supreme Court, raised two children, earned plenty of money, kept her marriage intact. Melissa ticks off these items, thinking: why does she work so hard? These thoughts depress her. What does her own future hold? What if she doesn't make partner? Will she ever find a man to love, be a mother herself? Frequently sleep overtakes Melissa as she asks herself these questions.

The Fast-Track Dilemma

Melissa is not alone. The pressure she feels to put in so many work hours that the rest of her life shrivels into nonexistence is shared by many in her profession. A report released by the Maryland State Bar Association in January 1989, found, in the words of its preface, "a pervasive malaise and a sense of dissatisfaction with the profession," which was directly linked to long working hours. A survey by the group of more than 1,000 lawyers revealed that 45 percent worked 50–59 hours weekly; 30 percent worked 60–69 hours; 13 percent worked from 40–49 hours weekly; and 6 percent worked 70 hours or more. Only 5 percent worked fewer than 40 hours weekly. One lawyer quoted in the study blamed the "high pace" mandated by the preoccupation with billable hours for "smothering other aspects of my life." This sentiment was seconded by Daniel F. Goldstein, a partner at Brown and Goldstein, a small Baltimore firm, who said, "The demands that lawyers impose on themselves are so stringent that the rest of their lives are in danger of atrophy."

But lawyers are not the only professional group feeling the time pressures arising from an excessive number of hours running on the fast track. Physicians, surgeons, scientists, college professors, and accountants all put in routinely very long hours. "Accounting professionals see extended hours as a real important issue," said Dan DeNisco, director of the Southeast Region for Robert Half International and Accountemps. "When accountants are in the middle of tax season, it's very common to work 60 to 65 hours during a week, and as you near the end of the week, things start getting fuzzy."

A recent Harris poll showed that, for all groups of professionals as well as for those who make $50,000 a year or more, the average workweek is slightly more than 52 hours. When Korn-Ferry surveyed 1,362 executives from Fortune 500 and Service 500 companies in 1985, it found the average workweek to be 56 hours. Moreover, the average workweek for all Americans (including commuting) is 47 hours per week—up from 41 hours in 1973. According to the Bureau of Labor Statistics, among 88 million Americans with full-time jobs in 1989, one out of four worked 49 hours or more a week on the job. Psychiatrist Joseph Ruffin of Oklahoma City has observed the physical effects of this dramatic increase in work hours and describes his patients as being "in a time-compressed state."

The time compression can be extreme. Not long ago I interviewed a hugely successful 31-year-old investment banker, a New York woman who earns more than two million dollars a year. She makes herself available to her CEO day and night, seven days a week. "It's all or nothing. You're always on. I've worked so many Christmases and New Years, I've been called back from vacations around the world, I've had the phone ring at midnight, at 3 A.M., saying the CEO wants me in L.A. for lunch the next day." She tosses clean underwear and a toothbrush in a bag and off she goes. She's kept up this pace for nearly a decade. "I couldn't tell you when my brother got married or my nieces and nephews graduated, but I know the exact date of almost every deal I made." She adds a bit ruefully, "I went from 19 to 30 overnight. I feel I've lost my twenties."

Perhaps no group of American workers, regardless of their jobs, feels the reality of this work-long-hours society as do mothers employed full-time, again a growing proportion of all mothers. Here is Stephanie's story—I found so many others similar to it that could have been told, but I was engaged by her in a special way.

Stephanie: Going Too Fast on the Mommy Track

Stephanie's day always begins the same way. The light on her closed eyelids wakes her up. She reaches over to turn off the alarm, her own internal clock so precise that she can tell the time without looking: 6:02 A.M. Still with eyes closed, Stephanie whips out her mental notepad and props it in front of her mind's eye: a blank sheet on which, every morning, she lists the things that must be done before she goes to bed that night. The list, always long, never contains anything she purely wants to do; everything is a must-do.

Somewhere near the tenth item, depression sets in. The persistent dull ache at the base of her skull asserts itself. The baby begins to cry, and Stephanie opens her eyes to check the clock: 6:02 exactly. The baby is awake a half hour too early. Stephanie nudges Steve, but his head stays buried deep in the pillow; he could be dead, except that he always sleeps this way.

The baby's insistent wail seems full of reproach. "Sometimes I wonder if the umbilical cord didn't get properly cut," Stephanie said to me wearily. "Anytime she cries, a tug in the pit of my stomach sends me bolting out of bed to get her." As she runs she is often seething because her husband won't go. Michelle stops crying when she sees Stephanie, who feels both cheered up and bathed in guilt—an emotional blend she's grown used to in the twenty months since Michelle's birth. Stephanie scoops the baby up and gets her ready to go. She figures things will improve once Michelle is toilet-trained and can get into nursery school.

Killer Commutes

Stephanie hates the horrible subject of day care, a constant worry-and-relief syndrome. After Michelle's birth, they found a day-care setup with a grandmotherly woman whose home smelled wonderfully of baking bread. Steve could walk there from his job and often had lunch with the baby. Back in those early months, Michelle was a real sweetie—smiles and giggles all the time. Unfortunately, it was a killer commute for Steve—one hour door-to-door in murderous traffic. He finally told Stephanie that he could hack the commute, but not with the added duty of day-care pickup and delivery on top of it. So they switched to a day-care home near Stephanie's workplace.

"Anything he can't hack," Stephanie told me, "gets dumped on me." Their current setup, at the home of a graduate student with a son and only one other child, is pretty good except that she's apt to phone them five minutes before they leave the house to say that she or her child is sick and they can't bring Michelle that day. This starts an immediate argument over who has to take the day off from work; usually Stephanie gives in.

No matter what she does—even if she wakes Steve up to watch the baby while she's in the shower, Stephanie notices her husband's reproachful look. "As if I'm not a good mother," she said. That makes her feel both annoyed and guilty, and she wonders if Michelle inherited her reproachful look from Steve.

At 7 A.M. the three of them leave the house. It will be at least 7 P.M. or as late as 9 P.M., if Steve works late, before they're together again. When Steve kisses her and the baby and waves getting into the car, Stephanie observes that he's glad to be free. She thinks about how she has deadlines coming up to get the magazine out, and how difficult it is to get out of the office in time to pick up Michelle. "I hate to feel sorry for myself," she admitted, "but sometimes I can't help it."

Stephanie checks the clock as she walks into the office: 8:00 on the nose most mornings. She is features editor at a monthly magazine in

Washington, D.C., no small feat given that every ambitious journalist in the country gravitates to D.C. Stephanie knows she's got talent, but she hates the daily pressure to perform. Much as she likes this company, Stephanie says it shows signs of being sexist. The top executives are men, and they just hired a new male editor—no female was even considered. More than that, she feels she's being monitored now that she's a mother: every day missed from work, although few and far between, every minute shaved off the clock, her unwillingness to put in overtime (as if she had a choice!), even her occasional flare of temper at the staff. Those things notch her down to the mommy track.

Setting a Demon Pace

Stephanie has decided that working at a demon pace is the only solution. She prides herself on outperforming every man in the shop. Despite the deadline pressure, she calls Steve on her hurried lunch hour whenever she feels guilty for her morning crankiness.

"I work hard at our relationship," she confided to me. "It scares me when I get stray thoughts of divorce." This is her second marriage and she's determined to make this one last. She considers her first marriage a black hole of lost time. "Nearly 10 years down the drain."

Now she's got a wonderful husband and child, but something is still missing. She and Steve both desperately want a second baby. Stephanie's mother died when she was only 10, and she was left with no siblings; she strongly desires that Michelle not be vulnerable to the lonely childhood she had. Steve, a child of a bitter divorce, still resents that his parents left him and their other children floundering. He talks earnestly to Stephanie about building a solid family that can withstand any blow.

But tension reigns in this area of their life, too. They've been trying for six months and she can't seem to get pregnant. At 35, Stephanie feels her biological clock ticking. It's made her cycle go awry; she never knows when she's going to get a period. She recently bought a test kit. If the test stick turns dark blue, that means you're going to ovulate within two days. Steve refuses to understand that it's best to wait for lovemaking until the dark blue appears. "Can we only make love on schedule?" he demands sarcastically, which makes Stephanie's stomach churn with anger. Her gynecologist explained that the sperm get stronger, increasing the chances of pregnancy. But Steve doesn't want to take responsibility; all he thinks about is what he wants.

Toward late afternoon, Stephanie always speeds up her work pace and glances repeatedly at the clock. Although she tries not to, she can't help calling her day-care mother. Not infrequently, she hears bad news. Michelle didn't eat her lunch, and her nose is running. Stephanie picks up the resentment in the other woman's voice: her son will likely come down with whatever sickness Michelle is getting. Minutes later, Stephanie barks a reprimand to a young editorial assistant who looks at her with hurt eyes. Stephanie has broken her prime rule of staff management: never call down anybody publicly. And here she stands, in the middle of the staff room, with everybody staring up from their terminals. Stephanie turns on her heel and exercises superhuman control by not slamming her office door.

At such times Stephanie sinks into a chair and raises her fingertips to throbbing temples. She knows things aren't easy for Steve either. He also wants to make it at his career. And he constantly assures her that everything is equal between them. He wants to be a good father as much as she wants to be a good mother.

Her Biological Clock

Stephanie perceives a difference between them which Steve can't understand. Time weighs on her in a way that it doesn't on him. Her years for motherhood are ticking away. She doesn't want to be a 42-year-old phenomenon like some celebrity moms. But the time factor enters in her career as well. Either she moves up, and soon, from features editor to managing editor, or she'll be relegated to the "mommy track" and never rise above her current level. If she has another baby now, how can she put in the time needed to win a promotion? And if she doesn't have another baby now—she'll be 36 at delivery if she conceives this month—how old will she be when her career permits another baby?

When Stephanie hits home at 7:20 P.M., exhausted, Michelle is whimpering and feverish. Stephanie calls out Steve's name but gets no response; it seems he always picks the worst nights to work late. The phone rings and it's Steve telling her not to wait up. She's the one who has to put the magazine to bed in two days, and with a sick child besides. In moments like this, Stephanie feels like screaming. She fixes a can of soup for herself and Michelle, then spoonfeeds the child. She gives her some liquid Tylenol and rocks her to sleep, hoping that she'll be all right in the morning. If she isn't, Steve will have to stay home this time and take her to the pediatrician.

Glancing down at the sleeping baby, whose hair is wispy and damp from the sweat which appears as her fever breaks, Stephanie is overwhelmed with love and remorse. How could she think about her stupid magazine deadlines while her angel is feeling miserable? Finally, Stephanie does what she's felt like doing all day: cries her eyes out with nobody there to see and judge her.

A Mother's Time Pressure

Stephanie's difficult set of time pressures is being faced by hundreds of thousands of working parents. The only people who face worse problems of time urgency are single parents, mostly mothers (one family in six is headed by a single mother), but sometimes fathers who must juggle the hours all by themselves. In the United States today, 57 percent of families are two-income families, and the majority of women with children work outside the home. More than 75 percent of these working women are in their prime childbearing years.

A study, in 1985, of 651 employees at a Boston corporation by Bradley Googins of Boston University's School of Social Work showed that married mothers averaged 85 hours a week on job, house, and child care and that married fathers averaged 66 hours. In a more recent poll commissioned by *Time* magazine and CNN, Yankelovich, Clancy and Shulman revealed that 73 percent of women and 51 percent of men complain of too little leisure time.

Sociologist Arlie Hochschild writes in *The Second Shift* (Viking Penguin, 1989), her recent book about working parents: "Adding together the time it takes to do a paid job and to do housework and child care, I averaged estimates from the major studies on time use done in the 1960s and 1970s, and discovered that women worked roughly 15 hours longer each week than men. Over a year, they worked an *extra month of twenty-four-hour days a year."* She concludes that most women work a "second shift" at home after they finish the first shift at their workplace.

She comments astutely, "As masses of women have moved into the economy, families have been hit by a 'speed-up' in work and family life. There is no more time in the day than there was when wives stayed home, but there is twice as much to get done. It is mainly women who absorb this 'speed-up.'"

But sometimes, in our speeded-up society, people become victims of time pressure when corporate forces descend on them through no fault of their own. Then the time trap closes on them, and gender makes no difference.

Wayne: A Manager Whose Time Has Run Out

Wayne didn't fall into a time trap. It dropped on his head. An easygoing man of 46 with a broad, open smile, Wayne is a family man who enjoys strong community ties and a wide circle of friends. Although he doesn't give the impression of being in a hurry, he seems quite dedicated to his job. His entire career has been spent with Sears, Roebuck & Co. in

Chicago. He joined the company straight out of college in the mid-sixties, starting as a management trainee. He moved upward at a steady pace in customer relations. Like clockwork, a promotion came along every couple of years.

"Right off the bat," Wayne told me, "I thought in long-range terms about Sears. I saw all kinds of possibilities for an exciting career."

Wayne's wife, Sharon, has felt as much a part of Sears as her husband. "Wayne was already working at Sears when I met him," she recalled. "During our engagement he got a promotion and we were both riding a crest. I've always gone to office parties, and Wayne brought people home socially. He brought his work home too—even his correspondence courses."

Anchored for Life

There was smooth sailing, with few ripples, for more than two decades. Wayne understood that he was party to a strong corporate covenant. "One thing about Sears," he explained, "if you had integrity, Sears would always have a place for you." Not that they promised you the CEO spot, but "you knew in your heart" you could stay a lifetime.

Sears was understanding. You didn't even have to be doing that good a job as long as you kept your nose clean. "Sears had a big, strong personnel department. You could go to somebody if you felt you weren't getting a fair shake," Wayne said.

By putting his heart into the job, Wayne personified the ideal employee: dedicated, honest, loyal. He fully expected to stay that way until retirement. When he moved to the spectacular Sears Tower in Chicago's downtown Loop in January 1975, both Wayne and Sharon felt anchored for life.

There seemed every reason to believe all his dreams could come true. The vast corporation provided a challenging career ladder that Wayne could climb to upper management. They bought a house in a pleasant western suburb, which made an easy commute by train—he could read, nap, relax on the trip back and forth. They put down roots in the community. The birth of their two daughters made things perfect. Theirs was a down-to-earth American Dream. Wayne and Sharon were enjoying the time of their lives.

The Year of Torture

But everything changed in 1988. Wayne's and Sharon's lives turned topsy-turvy. Sharon calls it "that year of torture when everybody was living in fear and terror." Rumors were rife: of takeovers, buyouts, white knights, poison pills, junk bonds, mergers, and a dozen other catch-phrases of a volatile corporate culture. There was even talk of selling the landmark Sears Tower. Wayne and Sharon lived in extreme tension as the rumors swirled. Nobody knew when the personnel cuts would occur, but everybody was saying, "It's going to happen, it's going to happen."

Sears was not forthcoming. Most employees got their information from the newspapers. Wayne said, "We knew for about a year there were definitely people who were going to get chopped. Then one day they had a big meeting to explain the total reorganization. They made an organizational chart with boxes labeling the job title, but no names in them. A couple of days later, the personnel manager called you in and told you whether you were in a box or not.

"The manager would say, 'Here's the box we have slated for you, or you can take the R.I. (Reorganization Incentive), which is the gobbledygook term for severance package,' Wayne said. "You got about a week to decide. There was absolutely no latitude. Many of the boxes people got slotted into were downsizing jobs—cuts in pay and title." He added, "They never published how many total cuts there were—I'd say 1,800 to 2,000 at headquarters in Chicago."

Feeling Powerless

The family suffered. As Sharon told it, "In June, before our vacation, Wayne was called in and told not to worry—a slot was there for him. We'd been through a couple of purges at Sears. It was only this last one that really scared Wayne. He felt seriously threatened. At first there was not pain, just discomfort. Then it built up. Sears is a rumor mill. You don't know how to filter out and get real information. All that time rumors were flying, the newspapers were our only source of information."

Sharon paused. "You'd get to a plateau for a while, then it was like standing on a table, and they'd take the legs out from under you. You felt powerless. You didn't have that much of a choice." I noticed how Sharon unconsciously switched from the first-person account to the more impersonal second-person as painful memories revived.

Wayne survived the 1989 bloodbath, but he knows that he isn't safe. The restructuring continues. More cuts will occur down the road, and he may be on the next list—six, twelve, or more months down the road. Time is at a standstill. Wayne feels his days are numbered at Sears; he's been reprieved, not saved.

Living on Slippery Ice

Sharon is devastated at the thought of pulling up stakes. Their children are in good schools, they belong to a wonderful church, have neighbors they can count on. Moreover, Sharon has been planning to earn a master's degree at Northwestern University, and have a real career. But what's the point of starting a program she might have to quit in six months?

Sharon initially tried to interpret the changes positively. She asked Wayne if his having survived the first cut means that he is slated to move up the reorganized corporation. Is he headed for bigger things?

Unfortunately, Wayne has explored that possibility and thinks not. In this first phase of the reorganization, he's been moved to a division which isn't profitable now and which exists in a fiercely competitive market. He figures this division will be closed down in a couple of years and he could get the ax then.

In about two years, Sears has announced that headquarters will move to a distant suburb, Hoffman Estates. Wayne and Sharon consider this location undesirable, but not as bad as losing his job. On the surface, they'll spend their time in the usual ways, but everything is different. The placid future that once lay before them has been snatched away. The time of their lives no longer belongs to them.

The reorganization at Sears has dramatically altered not only the long-term time lines of Sharon's and Wayne's lives, but also the day-to-day schedule and pace of work at the Tower. "Some people have responded by working themselves to death," Wayne remarked. "The guy I work for goes in every Saturday or Sunday. There are fewer people to get the same things done. We literally run out of time. There's just so much more to do. One guy goes in at three or four in the morning—he's crazy. He'd be there at 5:30 every morning if he could. The deadlines are the same. They've tried to streamline the work, cut out duplication, and so on, but there's still a certain amount of administration that's necessary.

"Many people work 10 to 12 hours a day," he continued. "A lot of people are taking the 5:30 A.M. trains into the city." They're reacting to their fears by increasing the pace and amount of work, believing they'll be assured of a future place with Sears.

But Wayne shakes his head. "There's no guarantee that strategy will work. We have no security now."

Broken Time Lines

In having their future plans disrupted by the corporation they considered almost a second family, Wayne and Sharon face a situation familiar to millions of Americans. Amanda Bennett, in her recent book *The Death of the Organization Man* (William Morrow, 1990), traces the forces that precipitated a dramatic reorganization of corporations over the past few decades, resulting in drastic reductions in the employee rolls of hundreds of companies. She points out, "From the beginning of 1980 to the end of 1987, an eight-year period, Fortune 500 companies dropped 3.1 million jobs, going from 16.2 million people at the end of 1979 to 13.1 million at the end of 1987." Moreover, the American Management Association recently reported that in the year ending in June 1987, 45 percent of its surveyed companies had cut staff; in 1988, 35 percent had downsized; in 1989, it was 39 percent. The association speculates that perhaps 45 percent of American corporations may cut staff early in this decade.

Downsizing is so widespread that it has led to a burgeoning of specialized employment agencies which counsel employees who get the ax as part of a corporate restructuring. "Downsizing has been like manna from heaven for the outplacement industry," said Jim Kennedy, publisher of the industry newsletter, *Consultant News*. "Our first directory was in 1980. There were 43 firms with estimated billings of $35 million a year." By 1986 the firms had nearly quadrupled, with total billings of more than $225 million.

As a major effect of this corporate revolution, many people have felt pressured to work longer hours—whether they wanted to or not. The studies indicating longer workweeks make laughable the predictions made in 1967 when testimony before a Senate subcommittee suggested that by 1985 people could be working just 22 hours a week or 27 weeks a year or could retire at 38. The big problem was supposed to be how to enjoy all that leisure time!

"On Wall Street in the 1960s, there was the theory of the paddling duck. An employee would slip into the office at daybreak, do a couple of hours' hard work and then go out for breakfast. He would amble back as his colleagues arrived and would glide through the day, impressing everyone with his effortless mastery of his chores. Today the worker would have nothing on anyone else. The executive suite and a lot of humbler domains beyond Wall Street have become seas of paddling ducks."—Peter T. Kilborn, *Tampa Tribune*, June 10, 1990.

There's a Way out of the Time Trap

Melissa, Stephanie and Steve, and Wayne and Sharon are among the dozens of people you will meet in this book. All of them feel driven, harried, or even tyrannized by time. As you probably noticed, there are differences in the way time pressure asserts itself, depending on age, gender, and circumstances. Wayne is a 46-year-old manager, Stephanie is a 35-year-old working mother, and Melissa is a 28-year-old single professional. Similarly, men and women in their twenties may feel the need to reach the peak of success by age 30. Women who are past 35 may hear the tick of the biological clock reminding them their time for motherhood is running out. And there are others who feel no internal time pressure, but perceive that outside forces, whether at work or at home, are pushing them to live at too harried a pace. Most time-pressured people, in any case, share an inexplicable sense of loss as well as the need to keep their feelings hidden.

As you read on, you will discover answers that apply to all these variations of time urgency. If you refuse to be squeezed by time pressures or tyrannized by the myriad of demands on your time, you can put effective solutions to work for you. You can put fun back in your life without sacrificing success. Time can become your friend and ally.

2

How People Fall
Victim to Time

Come what come may

Time and the hour runs through the roughest day.

SHAKESPEARE, *MACBETH*

Like most of us, Melissa did not start her career burdened by a sense of time urgency. She joined her prestigious law firm full of exuberance and confidence. Unencumbered by family obligations, or a serious relationship with a man, she had every expectation that she could easily attain the coveted post as junior partner. In her eagerness to succeed, and flushed with her early success as a brilliant attorney, she put in longer and longer hours until she woke up one day and realized that time pressures ruled her life.

Over the course of interviews with many successful people, I have often observed this pattern. Most people succumb as part of a barely noticeable process. Time, after all, is invisible. Subtle forces go to work—pressures both within and outside ourselves. We start out eager, certain that we can manage the long hours of a big job plus everything else in our lives. As time passes, more obligations get heaped on. Our enthusiasm dampens, but we're still willing. It may take several years before we confront the problem of time urgency. One day, for no apparent reason, we find ourselves not merely busy but overwhelmed by time urgency.

While I was doing my research, many people explained their sense of time urgency as stress from a relationship, or anxiety over job demands, or worry about a child's day care. And yet, expressions about time kept popping into the interviews. "I don't have time" became a refrain running through almost every account. When I pursued the issue of time in their lives, the answers were revelatory. Certain similarities kept appearing, regardless of the differences in circumstances among these men and women—from college students to physicians, from single professionals to working mothers. Perhaps most striking was their ability to pinpoint when time urgency hit them. This wasn't necessarily when it began, but when it crossed the threshold of their awareness. Many of them dated the problem back to their school days, sometimes even to grammar school.

Alex: A College Student Driven by the Academic Clock

A 20-year-old with a rugged athletic build, Alex has curly blond hair and an engaging grin. To the casual observer he seems very laid back, but this is a look he deliberately cultivates. The facts contradict his apparent ease.

"It's funny," he told me over a Coke in the snack bar at Johns Hopkins University, "but I can remember exactly when I first started to obsess about time. It was towards the end of my freshman year at Hopkins. Everything was cool the first semester, because they put all students on a pass/fail system here, so I did okay without having to put in too much effort.

"The heat was on from Day One the second semester, because that's when grades started to count. But I wasn't worried. I'd been a good student in prep school. Still, the pressure started to creep in. One night I had a bad dream and woke up in the middle of the night in a cold sweat. I suddenly felt swamped. All the due dates for papers started running through my mind. Then exams came crashing down on my head. I thought: My God, there's no way I can fit it all in!"

Alex's life had become an endless round of term papers, quizzes, class presentations, reports, each with a due date attached, with final exams at the end of the term looming as the dreaded monster. I asked him if the time pressures over his academic life interfered with his social life.

Alex grinned. "I'm fighting not to let that happen," he said. "I'm trying to make it an absolute rule: Come Friday night, no matter what's hanging over my head, I say forget it! I've got to relax!"

Lisa: A Grad Student Old before Her Time

When Lisa sat down in my office, I couldn't believe that the exuberant, 24-year-old woman before me, exuding energy and an intelligent self-possession, could refer to herself as concerned about being "old before my time." It seemed incredible.

"I was always conscious of time," she told me, "even as a small child. I noticed it passing, considered it precious, wanted to make the most of it. I felt that was natural. Both my parents are academics and we were a busy, highly motivated family. High academic standards were set for me, and I enjoyed attaining them. Some of my happiest memories are the intellectual discussions I had with my father in the kitchen as we did the dishes together.

"I felt I was on top of time all through school and through my college years. I was an honor student at an Ivy League school, Columbia University in New York City, and I enjoyed the competition. Ironically enough, it was when I went to grad school, in the sleepy town of Charlottesville with the bucolic rolling countryside, at the University of Virginia, that time urgency hit me like a ton of bricks.

"I walked into a graduate English class one day and I was shocked at the haggard faces of the other graduate students. The women had circles under their eyes, wore their hair tightly pulled back or any old way, and I thought, 'Is this going to happen to me?'"

From that day on, Lisa told me, she began to be constantly aware of the passing of time and of the shortened amount of time she had left to get her degree and start her career.

"I began to think I was getting old before my time, constantly checking myself out in the mirror, looking for the first gray hair or searching my forehead for a fine line or something that looked like an early wrinkle."

Lisa confessed that nothing essential has changed in her schedule— she isn't actually any more pressed for time than she was in her college years, but now her perception, her point of view, the way she regards the time lines of her life, has changed dramatically. She says that many of her friends in graduate school feel the same way, and none of them knows what to do about it. What distresses her the most is that her sense of time urgency seems to be getting worse.

When I asked why she thought this had happened to her, she paused. The question had never occurred to her. Then she said, with a shrug, "Maybe it's trying to make it big too soon."

Tony: Catching Himself as He Succumbs

Tony is a tall, handsome, single man in his early twenties, an Ivy League graduate with plenty of talent and ambition. He makes no bones about wanting to hit the top of the corporate ranks, where he feels the air is rarefied and golden parachutes are standard perks these days. But he's beginning to examine more closely the investment of time he's making in the corporation where he works.

"I'm a goal setter," Tony announced as we sat down together in his postmodern, hi-tech office. "I'd like to be an SVP [senior vice president] by my mid-twenties to late twenties. At first I told myself I was happy and fulfilled putting in 50-, 60-plus hours every week, arranging my weekends, in fact my whole life, around work and the company. I got lots of positive feedback, felt a tremendous high that I was getting noticed by the guys at the top. One day a memo of mine came back with a note on it from CEO. It said, 'Good work, Tony.' Terrific!

"But then I got to thinking. Do I picture myself going at this same pace in 10 years? Or 20 years? I realized there will always be someone coming along who's younger than myself, a little bit smarter, who got their college degree in less time from a better school. There will always be someone willing to put in more hours than I am. Then I realized I have to consider the possibility of a CBO [corporate buyout] or a hostile takeover."

Tony leaned forward earnestly. "This could mean that the goal I have defined myself by, measured my satisfaction by, is suddenly no longer a possibility. Where would I be left? After working so hard and competing fiercely for so long, I could be left out in the cold. I could be left devoid of a true self and hopelessly undefined as a person. I could discover that I placed too much stake in the climb."

The young man toyed with a pencil on his desk. Finally, he looked at me. "I've got to rethink my goals. I could end up a big loser if I keep going on like this."

They Hit the Fast Track Running: The Twenties

As soon as I began my round of interviews with college students, graduate students, and people in their early to mid-twenties who were new to the corporate environment, it became clear that time urgency was a taken-for-granted phenomenon among them. They are the post-baby boomers, a generation raised with time pressures. Many of them had to take competitive tests to get into the "right" private nursery school. Their parents put them on the fast track as soon as they were potty-trained. By the time this generation of the super-bright and talented were into second-year prep school, they were already taking their pre-SAT exams to measure their potential for getting into Princeton at least, if not Harvard or Yale. As a generation, they have been pushed by parents, hustled by guidance counselors, and warned of the competition by career development officers in college.

As the current graduates begin the decade of their twenties and move into the job market, they're already running. The young man I've called Tony was unusual among those I interviewed in that he was already raising questions about how much of his life he ultimately wanted to turn over to the corporation. Most people in their twenties could have been the younger brothers and sisters of Melissa. They want to make it, they've experienced time pressures for a number of years, and they believe that if they want to make it big, they have no choice but to get in harness and run as fast as they can. As I interviewed a number of them, I wondered if they felt this way precisely because they belong to an over-tested generation, programmed to perform from infancy.

As successors to the baby boomers in a belt-tightening economy, they don't feel automatically guaranteed of "having it all." They believe they must turn over great chunks of their time as the price of success. Fresh out of college or graduate or professional school, they start out willing to give their all. It's usually a few years down the road when time urgency becomes more than just a nuisance.

Ann-Marie: A Bank Auditor on Taut Time Lines

I had just finished teaching a two-day communications seminar to a dozen bank auditors in Oak Brook, Illinois, corporate home to many Fortune 500 companies. Ann-Marie, one of two women participants, approached me as I waited in the corporate suite for my ride to O'Hare airport. I had been impressed with her during the course. She had spoken softly and less often than her more aggressive colleagues, but with a serious and intelligent regard for her profession. Sitting beside me, she asked for advice about a problem that turned out to be time urgency.

Ann-Marie travels five days a week as a bank auditor, she told me, but that wasn't the problem which was affecting both her personal and professional lives. "At first I was managing everything beautifully. I held my own with the guys I work with," she said. "I'm a pretty competent auditor," she added matter-of-factly.

"But when I got married, I was at a disadvantage. Most of the staff are single guys who want to go out on the town at night after putting in very long days—they'll just crash when they go home on weekends. But I'm not interested in running around, so that makes me a bit of an outsider. I'm not part of the 'in' group, and I'm afraid this will count against me when it comes to promotions. Two guys at my level have recently been promoted. It's true that I did arrive at the bank shortly after them, and I've been told I'm the next one up for promotion, but I'm still worried.

"This is a great bank," she continued. "I already left another bank, although I was very happy in my work and had a terrific mentor there, because I had access to enough financial information to know the bank's condition was shaky. I don't want to keep job-hopping. I want to figure out how to make it here."

To protect her position, Ann-Marie works long hours during the week and finds herself exhausted every weekend. "I get depressed because I have housework, laundry, shopping, errands staring me in the face when I'd just like to relax. I don't feel like doing more work."

When Ann-Marie and her husband Felix got married, they agreed that everything would be 50-50 between them. Recently, however, a change has occurred in their lives which has upset the balance. Ann-Marie's husband, an engineer who wants to upgrade his skills as part of a strategy to reposition himself for the future, has begun work on his MBA. Felix argues that he has less "disposable" time than she does, so it's only fair that she take care of all the household chores—just until he gets his graduate degree, which could be two or three years from now.

"That seems fair enough," Ann-Marie said, "but I'm not happy this way. I don't know what we'd do if we had a baby. As it is, we have a dog that requires a lot of care, and it's always up to me."

She never wanted a marriage like her parents'. "My mother waited on my father hand and foot. He was king in our house." Ann-Marie's mother, now that the children are grown, works three jobs, still runs around like crazy. Ann-Marie thinks her mother works those hours to escape her father's demands. In any case, she refuses to repeat her mother's mistakes. She doesn't want to get less than her due—either at home or in her career.

But the time lines are starting to tighten up on both fronts. Somehow, the combined demands of her career and her husband have robbed Ann-Marie of personal time, pure do-nothing enjoyment time, and it is adversely affecting both her professional life and her marriage.

Donna: The Special Time Urgency of Mothers

In the course of my work as a communications consultant, I meet many talented professional women who are struggling to come to grips with the special time urgency of working mothers. It's twofold: the inner biological clock, which determines the time limit to the possibility of motherhood, and, once a mother, the enormous, unlimited time demands created by the presence of an infant. Regardless of how superbly the day-care problem may be solved, the young mother feels the visceral pull of her child seven days a week, from morning to night.

Not long ago I spent several days teaching a group of senior vice presidents at a major bank in Newark, Delaware. I took the occasion to interview the training director when we ate lunch together in the pleasant atrium of the executive dining room. Her story resembles those of numerous other bright women who must face the problems that occur when personal and career lines come into conflict.

Donna, a crisply stylish and competent woman in her early thirties, described the ambience of the bank as upbeat and friendly, but with a very fast working pace. "Tomorrow isn't good enough—it has to be now," she said of her supervisor's expectations. The bank has posted time goals for every function, along with the percentage of employee attainment: 21 seconds to answer the phone, always by the second ring, as a small example. This creates a heady atmosphere of speed.

I asked Donna how many hours people put in there, and she replied, "Sixty hours a week—that's taken for granted."

Now that she is the mother of an 11-month-old baby, things have changed for Donna. "I used to put in 60, even 70 hours a week. I loved my work. But there were days when I said to myself, 'I'm sinking, I'm sinking. I'm not going to come up this time.' I don't put in those hours anymore. I put in 40 hours. But I feel I can keep up my performance."

On the several days when I was present, however, her schedule belied her description. One morning she arrived at 7:30 A.M. amid a torrential downpour, having first deposited her baby in day care. I wondered what time she had gotten up, for she was impeccably groomed and her suit tastefully accessorized. She mentioned that unexpected changes required her to come in early, but she was surely putting in lots more than 40 hours that week.

Donna is clearly ambitious to move up in the organization. She believes she won't be penalized as long as she can keep her performance up to the standards of those who put in 10 or 20 more hours than she does every week. But can she? As one human resources executive put it to me, "In today's corporation, you must not only be competent, you must be *perceived* as competent by those above you." Donna is vulnerable, especially in a corporate environment where sheer presence is a large measure of employee performance. Her shorter workweek could easily be interpreted as a less than first-rate performance.

Tangled Time Lines

The special time problems of working women with small children are being experienced all across corporate America today. William, a senior vice president at the same bank where I interviewed Donna, told me that corporate management was aware of problems arising because of its aging workforce. By "aging," William meant that a majority of employees currently in their twenties were edging toward their thirties. Senior management recognized that, as employees married, settled down to buy a house, and contemplated having a child, they weren't as willing to be at the disposal of the company. The bank was trying its best to respond appropriately. A day-care center was being planned on-site. Amenities such as a first-rate cafeteria and a fitness center were already in place. Company picnics for the whole family and children's fairs were annual treats.

But as of now, William said in response to my query, the company has no intention of lowering its expectations of the typical 60-hour work-week. The harried pace will go on, except when the family joins in for social events on a few occasions every year. Women will have to address the day-to-day time problems on their own, as well as the thorny issues of career advancement versus maternal satisfaction.

Robbing Peter to Pay Paul

For working parents, time urgency may be severe. The usual response pattern is a juggling act among tasks and demands that must be met. Most parents end up robbing Peter to pay Paul, a catch-up game that is never won. Once we've achieved maximum speed at our daily pace and find that we still don't have time to meet all the demands being placed on us, we tend to shorten our personal "time line" in order to lengthen our work "time line." And Arlie Hochschild, in her study of working parents, *The Second Shift*, found that women most often bear the brunt of increased time pressures in the family, sacrificing common personal pleasures—"and most did it willingly."

Do People Consider Time with Family Important? A recent national survey of 1,200 people, on behalf of Massachusetts Mutual Life Insurance Corporation, uncovered some startling facts. It found that nearly two out of every three people—63 percent—listed the family as their best source of pleasure. Yet despite the family's importance to them, 66 percent felt that the quality of family life in America is fair to poor. The reason, according to 35 percent, is that parents don't have enough time to spend with their families. And 46 percent said they don't spend enough time with family. And yet, when respondents were offered a hypothetical job that would take more time away from the family but would give a 15 to 35 percent increase in pay, or simply more prestige, two out of every three respondents said they would be likely to take the job. In fact, 36 percent said they would be very likely to take it. On a scale going from very likely to very unlikely, not a single one of the 1,200 respondents said he or she would be very unlikely to take the job.

Although most people succumb gradually to time urgency as responsibilities accumulate, that is not the only way it can happen. Sometimes a sudden massive weight of family responsibility drops down on a person's shoulders accompanied by crushing time demands. Given the mobile and fragmented structure of families today, with individual members scattered at wide distances apart, the burden may hit one person in the family with overwhelming force.

Jason: Swamped by Time Demands of Elderly Parents

Jason spent very long hours at his job as city desk editor at a major metropolitan newspaper. He often brown-bagged it for lunch, then went to a nearby fast-food restaurant for supper. But he didn't mind. He was in his late twenties, unattached, new to town, and eager to move up the ladder as a journalist. He coveted a Pulitzer Prize some day. Deadline pressure didn't bother him because he happily gave all the time he had to a job he loved.

Then disaster struck. He answered the phone one day at the newspaper office and gave out a shout that made everyone in the newsroom jump: His mother had been struck down by a stroke. His father, already an invalid beset by financial problems, decided with Jason's mother to move to the city where Jason worked. There was no other alternative. In that moment Jason went from being happily busy to being time-driven. He had to locate living quarters and doctors, arrange for movers, consult lawyers about his family's financial problems, fly to his hometown in Massachusetts to help his folks pack up and move.

That was only the beginning. When they arrived in town, Jason's mother constantly called him at the office. His time literally was no longer his own. Work piled up. Since he was already used to putting in 10- or 12-hour days, he had little time left for his parents. Jason felt swamped.

Kathy: Overwhelmed by Needs of Her Widowed Mother

"I'd do anything in the world for my mother," Kathy confided to me earnestly. She was a pretty blond woman, vivacious and eager to please. "After my dad died, Tom and I drove to Youngstown almost every weekend to help Mom through her bereavement. Most of the time we took the kids—Sarah was only a baby then, and Billy was just three. Once, Tom went down by himself for a few days to paint the house. But Mom had a hard time making up her mind what she wanted to do—leave the old house and come live near us in Cleveland, or stay put. The trips back and forth wore me down. After two years, she finally decided to move.

"We found her an apartment," Kathy continued, "and I was so relieved she would be nearby. I thought my troubles were over. Was I wrong! On the morning Mom arrived, Billy had a high fever with bronchitis, and there I was, on a freezing winter day, sitting in the car with a sick kid, waiting in front of the apartment building for the moving van. It went downhill from there. I felt like a rag doll, pulled in opposite directions. My mother needed me full-time, and so did my young children, plus I had a part-time job that had to be squeezed in. I couldn't keep up. It was like a nightmare every day."

Kathy went, overnight, from being a busy but contented young mother to a harried mother/daughter who could never seem to catch her breath. Among the millions of people in Kathy's generation, the baby boomers— the majority of whom are in the prime of their careers—there are many who must shortly face the added time responsibility of elderly parents. As one top human resources executive remarked to me, "In another ten years the baby boomers will be known as 'the grieving generation.'"

Frank: A Surgeon Whose Wife Left Him

Frank was chief of staff at a major medical center in Illinois, his long days filled to capacity. His tremendous zest for surgery kept him on top of the world, despite his bone-wearying hours, not only because he loved his profession and got tremendous satisfaction from the praise of his colleagues, but because he had a wife who seemed like a throwback to the fifties: she kept everything running perfectly back in their suburban dream home. He was oblivious to domestic details; Mary was a marvel. A model mother as well, she took care of their two children and never troubled Frank about anything.

Then one day Mary left him for another man. In a state of shock, Frank fell into a tailspin. There was suddenly just one person to do what two people had done up until yesterday. To the neighbors in his bucolic suburb, Frank seemed like a madman, frantically rushing to find baby sitters, chauffeurs, cleaning help, launderers, errand runners, a corps of hired hands to do the mind-boggling variety of tasks that used to be handled by Mary. Frank was dumbfounded. He couldn't grasp that his life had fallen apart overnight. His time had run amok.

The Myth of Invincibility

In the ancient myth of Icarus, the young man grew so enchanted with his sense of soaring power and delight that he convinced himself (despite his father's warnings) that he was invincible. No harm could come to him, for he was capable of daring any height successfully.

This same illusion overtakes many successful people. As the forces within us (the desire for high achievement, the wish to please loved ones, the need to be dutiful) and those outside us (job requirements, community requests, society's pace) combine to make us continually pressed for time, we react by telling ourselves we can do whatever we must. That reaction is ingrained in our "can-do" American culture. Then we mythologize ourselves: we can go faster and faster every millisecond of each day, impervious to weakness or fatigue. We can do it all and have it all because we are invincible.

Even if we admit to ourselves, as Stephanie and Melissa do, that time pressures are weighing us down, we endeavor to keep this hidden from others. We dread appearing before others as less competent, less successful, less in control than we really are. Part of the power image we project to our bosses and colleagues at work is that we can handle any task handed to us. The faster we go, the harder we run, the more important we prove ourselves to be.

Another Myth: The Time Management Solution

Time management techniques aren't a panacea. They've been praised as the ultimate solution for busy people since Alan Lakein wrote his classic book, *How to Get Control of Your Time and Your Life* (NAL, 1973). These techniques are useful for time wasters and procrastinators, but I've observed that most people suffering from time urgency belong in neither category. To the contrary, successful people are usually well organized and make efficient use of their time. As an early reaction to escalating time pressures, they frequently increase their use of time management techniques. Melissa and Stephanie, for example, both employ these strategies routinely: working on two or more tasks at once; making "to-do" lists; following a schedule down to the quarter hour; scanning their daybooks for more "time slots" for chores.

But the result is that more demands continue to fill up the empty spaces created by these efficiency methods. If by a miracle they could suddenly have a 30-hour day, it would still not be enough. Time literally fills their lives—every nook and cranny, every extra space. The techniques of time management can actually exacerbate the problems of time-driven people rather than help them.

The theory behind all time management books is a view of time as a line extending in space which can be divided into numerous segments or "bytes" of time, each of which can be made productive. To increase productivity, the segments are chopped into smaller pieces, with each one filled more productively. Carried to the extreme, we get compressed time: the 90-minute hour, the multiple-task minute, even the busy subconscious mind working away our sleep time.

The Last Two Myths

Time urgency causes misery. When people spontaneously confided their distress to me, my response was to move on to ask them how they were trying to get rid of their time pressures. But I discovered to my surprise that despite their suffering, they put up barriers to a solution. The two reactions I've heard most often amount to little myths. The first is: "Time pressure is normal—everybody has it." The logic is faulty, of course; every citizen of the United States could have a certain trait, which would not make it automatically normal. But to feel that way creates an obstacle. You can't overcome a problem unless you look for a solution.

The second myth is: "I've got no choice. This is the way it has to be." The most common reason people then went on to give for why it had to be that way at work is: "The job requires it. If I don't put in these long hours, somebody else will, and I'll lose my job." For time pressures stemming from their personal life, they said, "There's nobody else to do it. If I don't do everything, nobody else will." These last two myths are refuges of the depressed and the downhearted, those who are fast losing ground in their daily battles with time.

Six Traits of Time-Pressured People

As I pursued my research, a pattern of time distortion began to appear among the people I interviewed, and the features of Urgency Addiction began to take shape. It became clear that a cluster of interrelated feelings, attitudes, and behaviors together describe the presence of time urgency. Some basic traits emerged as fundamental: Persistently feeling harried, pressured, or driven by time; feeling constrained by time pressures; having a strong impulse to hurry; being preoccupied with the passage of time; engaging in a constant struggle for control of time; being gripped by worry over lack of time; having one's thoughts or feelings dominated by an awareness of time; forcing oneself into a speeded-up pace; feeling that there is not enough time.

Although Urgency Addiction appears in varying degrees and ways, it can be expressed in six traits. Most people who suffer from time urgency:

1. Monitor Time Excessively. In talking with people pressed by time, I discovered that if you spend even a short period with them, you can observe how closely they monitor the passing of time. A clock or watch must always be nearby. Although they have very different personalities, lifestyles, and responsibilities, Melissa and Stephanie, for example, share certain obvious habits: They live by schedules, broken down to the quarter hour; they check their watches and clocks incessantly; they feel pressure to fit more work into smaller segments of time. They rely heavily on calendars, lists, schedules. In fact, they keep multiple lists and follow their schedules religiously, managing time to the point where no 10-minute period in the day is unaccounted for. They all, without exception, exhibit time-keeping dependency on clocks, watches, and schedule books.

2. Go at Too Fast a Pace. Everybody feels comfortable at a different pace, and this pace naturally varies from day to day and place to place. But people who are time-driven push themselves at a pace that goes beyond their own comfort zone. Certain physical gestures betray this form of time urgency: Drumming fingers, darting and scanning eyes, short attention span, inability to concentrate on the subject at hand, shifting feet, fast walking everywhere, tics, speeding up activities, inability to relax; restlessness; intolerance for waiting in line. Some people who live at a souped-up pace display anger at stoplights or supermarket checkout counters if there is even minimal delay—as if they've put their internal motors into high gear and can't bear to pause even for a minute.

3. Acquiesce in All Time Demands at Work. In our fast-paced, highly competitive society, where talk of global competition now dominates our workplaces, workers correctly feel both spoken and unspoken messages to put in longer and longer hours. Melissa responds to her law firm's requirements of 1,700 billable hours by putting in workweeks of 55 hours or more. Wayne reacts with panic in the face of corporate restructuring that may result in time running out for him. They spend more time at work than seems balanced or proportional to their overall lifestyles, and yet they are reluctant to refuse any time demands put on them in the workplace. If it becomes an issue with loved ones at home, that is a sure sign that work has become the focus of time urgency.

4. Give Up Personal Time. This is an act of self-deprivation. In a frantic effort to meet the time demands of her job, her baby, her husband and home, Stephanie—like many working mothers—has, little by little, given up all private time for herself. The same is true of Melissa, for whom work replaces a whole personal life. Melissa seems to be working entirely for herself, but in reality her waking life is given over almost exclusively to her law firm. She has suppressed large parts of her personality, depriving herself of all identity except that of attorney-on-the-fast-track. Ann-Marie, the bank auditor, resents the intrusion into her leisure time and is trying to fight it. The same is true of Donna, the young mother and training director who finds herself with conflicting time lines. But for both of them, the time pressures at work and at home are combining to threaten the loss of their personal time.

5. Lose the Ability to Enjoy the Present Moment. Stephanie fails to enjoy her activities as they present themselves to her because her attention is always focused on the endless list of future tasks that spreads before her each day. Stephanie is also unable to enjoy the present moment because she feels weighed down by the past and its disappointments, for which she is trying to compensate. Melissa forever casts her net into the future—looking for the next client, planning the next brilliant move, anticipating her role as junior partner. She can rarely rest easy in the moment she is living. Kathy, the harried young mother with a widowed mother to help, also fails to enjoy the present moment because she feels burdened by the next request that could come at any time. So, too, with Jason. Because of the crushing burden that has descended on him with the arrival of his elderly parents, he can no longer enjoy his work. Editorial tasks are viewed not as challenges to savor, but as onerous duties that never seem to get finished. Wayne finds his present completely overshadowed by worry for the future: What will happen to him, he wonders as he goes through his workday? Lisa, the graduate student, had the ability to enjoy the present moment one day and found it gone the next!

6. Possess an Inadequate Sense of the Future. Virtually everyone who suffers from an excessive sense of time urgency postpones fulfillment of desires and goals into an indefinite future. Melissa dreams of taking time off, but repeatedly sets a later date for herself. Many people suffering from time urgency regard the future as a taskmaster whose demands can never be met. Stephanie feels at the mercy of outside forces: her baby, day-care homes, job demands, and so on. Wayne and Sharon, although not governed internally by a sense of time urgency, feel that their future has been taken out of their hands and that they must live from day to day. The thought of time passing makes them feel insecure. What is typical of all of them is an inability to rest easy in the unfolding of the future. They are continually looking ahead to duties and tasks, but not to possible pleasures. As Lisa put it, "I've lost my childhood pleasure in anticipation—now I look forward with dread to the future."

What's at the Bottom of It All: Time Distortion

Time urgency is more than a personal behavior pattern. It is close to being a dominant feature of our culture. John Robinson, head of the Americans' Use of Time project at the University of Maryland, reports that people feel they don't have enough time to fit in all the things that must be done. Repeated Harris polls have shown that people feel over-burdened by having too much to do in too little time. One recent survey revealed that the amount of leisure time enjoyed by the average American has shrunk 37 percent since 1973. In his book *Time Wars* (Henry Holt, 1987), social theorist Jeremy Rifkin maintains "that in a culture so committed to saving time we feel increasingly deprived of the very thing we value."

Being time-pressured is not the same as being busy. People who are happily busy aren't pressed by time, nor do they experience all the traits described above. Being busy is a factual statement, one not invested with the feelings that accompany Urgency Addiction. What I gradually discovered, in observing and interviewing scores of people, is that the underlying phenomenon of Urgency Addiction is an actual and fundamental distortion of one's sense of time. It happens when being busy yields to a feeling of being pressed or harried by time. Those entities to which we assign the names "past," "present," and "future"—believing we know exactly what we're referring to—have somehow lost their natural meaning. But this becomes clear as we take a look at those who are so deeply immersed in time urgency that we can call them time addicts.

3

WHAT HAPPENS WHEN PEOPLE TRY TO OUTRUN TIME

O for an engine to keep back all clocks!

—BEN JONSON

There is no antidote against the opium of time.

—SIR THOMAS BROWNE

Time urgency causes misery. Even mild degrees of time pressure create discomfort in people, robbing them of the day-to-day pleasures in life. As I got deeper into my research, talking to more people from various walks of life, it struck me that not only is there a widespread cultural problem of time urgency, there are many degrees of suffering. Some people are affected so pervasively that their entire lives are given over to obsessive concerns with the passage of time. The story that follows describes a man whose devotion to work and whose bonding with his computer seemed to consume his every waking moment.

David's Story: Clocking His Life in Milliseconds

Until recently David was a money manager at one of the top Wall Street brokerage houses, his annual earnings around $250,000. Now he's gone independent. He took the occasion of the 1987 Wall Street crash to strike out on his own. Without much trouble he acquired a hot list of clients whose money he invests. He trades at a fierce pace, having lured these clients to himself by promising returns of 20 to 22 percent. But David isn't worried. Living on the edge, working the spectrum of stocks and securities, he knows he's terrific. Not 30 years old, and on his way to the top.

On an ordinary day David racks up dozens of calls; he never gets through lunch without a few, even when he's got a potentially important client with him. First thing he does on entering a restaurant is to check

35

out the phones—his connection to the action when he can't be on the computer. That receiver attached to his ear, cradled on his shoulder, nuzzled to his cheek, brings him a warm rush.

One day when I joined David and a new client for lunch, he slid out of the booth as soon as we were handed menus.

"Be right back," David said, already shouldering his way through the lunch-hour crowd, toward the phones. After a period in which his client and I made small talk, he came gliding back, grinning ear to ear, as high as if he'd just been shown how to walk on air.

"Doing deals, doing deals. What'll you have?" David said. But I could almost feel his mind racing ahead to his next connection: If it falls together right, he's got a fantastic deal.

Before David and his new client left the restaurant, the client entrusted him with a large portfolio. They shook hands outside. "I've got all the confidence in the world in you, David," he said.

David grinned, but his eyes were scanning the traffic. He hopped a taxi, eager to check out the computer action: What's happened in the 90 minutes he's been gone from his desk?

Back at the office, David flips through his phone messages and tosses them aside as he sits down at his terminal. His fingers fly over the keyboard. The screen fills up with numbers. David stares intently, then relaxes. He's plugged in again, and all's right with the world. The ticker tape is from the dinosaur age. It tells you that IBM is selling at $109. So what? That could be IBM an hour ago in the New York market. What David cares about is now. He's got to know what's happening this instant *in all the markets globally.*

David itches to find the gap in what the stock is selling for, from one market to the next. If it's there, he zooms into the gap, picks up the phone and does a deal. He could make a fortune—or lose one—in the time it takes to go to the washroom.

At 30 seconds before 2 P.M., David's on the phone again and makes his all-important connection. He talks a blue streak, working the keyboard like lightning. In a few minutes, he's done a deal, and the adrenaline rushes through him—a rush better than sex, better than cocaine. He jumps to his feet, whistles, paces around the room, grins at his secretary, lights a cigarette. He's high! At this moment, he feels lighter than air.

The Computer Is His Lifeline

Within a minute David hits his computer again; it's more than family, lover, and best friend rolled into one. The computer is his lifeline, which explains why he is always on the lookout for the newest model—whether for office, home, or travel. A new generation is constantly being hatched. He's crazy about his newest laptop—an airport-friendly baby that weighs in at only 4.4 pounds and measures 1.4 inches thick—an easy fit into his briefcase. Its access time is as fast as 5 milliseconds, with a shorter stroke keyboard to save time too. These facts matter because David clocks his life not in days, hours, or even minutes, but in milliseconds and nanoseconds.

After several more hours at the office terminal, David heads for home. By the time he gets stuck in a traffic jam on the Long Island Expressway, he sags with a brief spell of fatigue. He considers using his car phone, but he sometimes gets static and can't hear a quotation; that makes him crazy.

David has been thinking about a move to the West Coast, figuring to get faster action there. The market is always open somewhere: London, Paris, Tokyo, Hong Kong. He could wake up at 3 or 4 A.M. and catch the last hour of action from Hong Kong. While having breakfast he could do some deals over the phone, and by the time he got to his office around 5 A.M., he could phone New York as it opened. By 9 A.M. New York time, he would already have done half a day's work on the West Coast.

But it looks like he won't have to move to get this kind of action. The markets are opening up. Globalization is getting to be more than a buzzword. More than that, the New York Stock Exchange, for the first time in its two-hundred-year history, has announced plans to begin after-hours trading soon and nighttime trading in 1991. Better still, the new trading will be conducted electronically, away from the trading floor. The Chicago Board Options Exchange, the Cincinnati Stock Exchange, and Reuters announced plans to build the world's first electronic network for 24-hour trading of stocks and stock options. The same thing is happening with Chicago's futures exchanges. Globex, developed by Reuters and the Chicago Mercantile Exchange, accesses commodity futures contracts trading 24 hours a day, and the Chicago Board of Trade, the world's largest futures market, has come up with its system, Aurora. David finds the 24-hour market the most exciting prospect in his life. He's learned to go on only four or five hours of sleep at night, getting ready for it.

Basically, David has everything he wants: a luxurious home, a Ferrari, a Manhattan condo, clothes, women, everything. And he's sought after. Both men and women fawn over him. But his restlessness prevents him from feeling satisfied; he has to be on the move. When he enters a room, he scans it as if it were a giant computer screen. He moves through the room with a vacant expression, nodding to people, carrying a drink in one hand. More often than not, he leaves a party without ever having sat down.

The last thing David does every night is to sit down for a few minutes at the PC in his bedroom and check out the action. His new Japanese model has a specialized microprocessor that uses speed-enhancing techniques known as reduced instruction set computing (RISC) methods. Its super-fast memory chip, at 100 nanoseconds, gives him zero-wait-state memory reads—a real pleasure.

David suffers from extreme time urgency not because he gets excited about computers which cut memory access from 20-billionths of a second to 10-billionths. What marks David as a victim is his fanatical determination to speed up time. While submitting to the tyranny of time urgency, he deludes himself that he is controlling time. His obsessive behavior resembles that of an addict. His wardrobe of computers amounts to little more than paraphernalia for making a connection with a world where no time lags exist. His life has assumed the same unreality as the computer environment in which time is measured in milliseconds and nanoseconds. David is an extreme example of a segment of the American workforce. There are others like him.

Marty: A High-Flying Californian

Marty, a young Californian, has been working for a year on an exciting project with a venture group parented by a major hi-tech corporation. At first it was the most wonderful opportunity he could imagine. He escaped the dull rules and routine of the corporation and joined a group of people like himself: bright, creative, spontaneous, inner-directed, innovative. In the early days of this newstream project, Marty and his colleagues were fired up with excitement. They all put in many extra hours voluntarily. They would arrive at work early in the morning to do calisthenics or fuss with their equipment. They held endless meetings: Marty came in to work most Saturdays, then sometimes on Sundays. The team developed a super camaraderie.

Marty's wife complained about his long hours, his growing moodiness at home, and his constant state of distraction. He paid little attention to her because the project kept him in a cocoon, shielded from everything else.

Unexpectedly, as the project neared completion, with every expectation of success, Marty began to feel tired, lacking the exhilaration he had expected. He faced the future—going back to the parent company with a conventional routine of 45 to 50 hours a week instead of 60-plus, with dread. In giving so much of his time to the venture group over the past year, he has lost touch with his family, friends, and himself as well.

What has happened is that the demands of the company, the project, and enthusiastic coworkers together served as the powerful external pressure on Marty to put in excessive numbers of hours. Add to that the internal pressure he put on himself—his ambition, excitement, intellectual curiosity, and keen competitiveness—and they all combined to stimulate him to work extremely long hours while putting everything else in his life "on hold" in the background. The mix of external and internal pressures created a tremendous energy, but the result at the end of a year was a feeling of self-depletion. Marty was suffering from time urgency in its extreme form.

Paul: Under the Gun Five Days a Week

Paul is a fortyish executive who works in the global economy. He runs a multinational conglomerate, contracting for the manufacture of top-quality sound systems.

Working according to global time, Paul puts in incredibly long hours during the week, but reserves every weekend without fail for himself and his wife. He suffers from extreme time pressure, but he convinces himself that he is in control by having one or two inviolable rules about time.

"Paul will not take business calls on weekends," says his wife Barbara. That is one of his inviolable rules, and to make sure he doesn't violate it, they take off every weekend—winter, spring, summer, and fall—for their home near Starlight, Pennsylvania. I asked them if they feel that the kind or quality of time they spend together in Pennsylvania is better than their time together during the week in New York City, and they both said yes unequivocally.

But Barbara points out that the getaway is only partial because Paul can't get work out of his mind. Starting out in their Mercedes from their condo in Riverdale, New York, they head up the Sawmill River Parkway to Tarrytown, cross the Tappan Zee Bridge, then ease into the foothills of the Catskills. "All the way to Pennsylvania, we talk about his work," she says. And they keep talking about his work when they arrive that night.

"Then the next morning we continue talking about his work at breakfast. Often it isn't until Saturday afternoon that his time is really free."

As I listened to Barbara describe her husband, he sounded all too much like myself when I was in the iron grip of time urgency. On those weekend getaways my husband and I used to take with the children, I would talk obsessively in the front seat about work as the children begged (unsuccessfully!) for my attention from the back seat. "Mommy, Mommy, listen," they would say, but I was still living in work-time and couldn't hear what they wanted to tell me.

In contrast, Barbara is a time-integrated person. She works as an administrator for a small accounting firm, where the atmosphere is busy but laid-back. "If I feel like taking a two-hour lunch and going to have my nails done, that's what I do," she comments. "Nobody is keeping track of my time. They like me and I like them. Of course they know I'll be responsive when something has to get out under a tight deadline."

Paul says he procrastinates and wastes a lot of time, but Barbara disagrees. "You are in *total* control of your time, Paul," she retorts vehemently. Then she turns to me.

"He gets home late every night. As soon as he sits down on the sofa, he falls instantly asleep. Sometimes he'll say he's got some reading to do and go into the bedroom. I'll go in later to see if I can do anything for him, get him a bite to eat, and I'll find him sound asleep."

Paul doesn't want to talk about the possibility that his time has gotten out of control. He freezes up when I try to probe the subject. Instead, he tells me about his second inviolable rule. "When I'm working, I won't take calls from anybody except my family. You've got to understand what's important in this life. If somebody from the family calls, my staff knows I'll take that call no matter what."

Both Paul and Barbara agree that to stop and analyze how one spends time is inevitably to confront oneself and one's life. "And that's scary," he remarks.

Larry and Diane: Time Pressures Change Lives

When I returned in early spring to do an in-depth interview with Diane and Larry, whom I had first interviewed six months before, I expected to find Larry in a mellow mood, enjoying some well-deserved leisure. He had been working long, hard hours as a developer, building up a business in a booming area of Montgomery County, Maryland, ever since he and Diane were married 18 years ago. Now there was finally a slowdown in the construction business—so much so that Larry and his partners had laid off about 25 percent of their workforce. But Larry wasn't worried that the building recession was anything more than a temporary dip which would soon correct itself.

So I was immensely surprised to find him with a full-blown case of time urgency. Gray hairs were sprouting in his brown hair, but even more obvious were the dark circles of fatigue under his eyes, and the darting, distracted expression they now had acquired.

"What's with Larry?" I asked Diane privately. "Isn't he taking it a bit easy these days?"

"Far from it," she said. "He's working harder than ever now—at least 70 hours a week. It's just that the kind of work he's doing now is different. Before, when the business was booming, he couldn't keep up with all the demands of the clients to get work out and projects finished. Now he's under a different kind of pressure—to go out and sell new business, to get enough projects to keep busy the people they haven't laid off. He used to have lots of night meetings, to get building projects approved by town councils and planning boards. Now it's more getting on the phones all day and trying to drum up business. If anything, he puts in longer hours."

Diane describes the time pressure her husband lives with due to his seven-day workweek. "Larry is already late before he wakes up in the morning." Even on Easter weekend, Saturday morning at 9 he was at a neighboring municipality to walk the grounds of a 2,000-acre parcel with the town council to persuade it to okay the development project. On Easter Sunday, between courses of a big extended-family dinner, Larry's partner called and they spent half an hour talking business. In the corner of the kitchen, near Diane's desk, is a briefcase bulging with papers and, on top of that, a thick stack of computer printouts.

"That's Larry's guilt package," says Diane. "He doesn't feel so bad about not being at work over the weekend, or coming home early during the week, if he has his pile of work along with him. That way if he gets a spare half hour, he'll do something."

Diane regards her husband as a man unable to relax. I observe him on a Saturday night when the whole family is at home, prowling about the house, puttering, looking for the tripod he'll need the next day for family photos. "Come on, sit down, Larry," says Diane repeatedly. "See, this is what I'm talking about," she tells me. "He can't relax."

When they're driving up to their condo in the Poconos or perhaps to their cottage at Rehoboth Beach in Delaware, Diane will be talking to him. Suddenly, he'll reach for his dictaphone and speak into it for a few minutes. "I know he can't be listening to what I'm saying—he's thinking about work," Diane says.

But Larry interjects, "That's how I get my mind free. If I can get those thoughts down when they pop up, then I can stop thinking about it." Diane comments, "It's very hard to get Larry away from the job. But if we do take a vacation—like our recent 10-day trip to Alaska with the children—then Larry has to work doubly hard before he goes and after he comes back, and it takes half the vacation time at the beginning for him to unwind."

Competing for Time

Diane blames herself for the fact that Larry's time at home is taken up with work. "I'm the one who kept complaining that he wasn't home enough, spending time with the family," she says. "So he comes home, but one way or another, the work has to get done. The children and I compete for his time when he's home—Saturday afternoon it's sports with Larry junior, but then Chrissy and I want time with him too.

"When he does come home for supper, he'll spend time with us. But inevitably, about 10 o'clock, after the kids are in bed, he'll take the tablecloth off the kitchen table and open up his briefcase. Sometimes he'll sit there till 1 or 2 o'clock in the morning. If he comes in late and sits in front of the TV, he'll immediately fall asleep."

I ask Diane if Larry has any time for himself, when he's not working. She thinks for a minute. "The only time Larry is alone, with time all for himself, is when he goes deer hunting, and he's up in a tree, at a deer stand," she says. "I asked him once what he thinks about when he's all alone up there, and he said he thinks about work there too"—Diane flashes me a wry grin—"but he says it's a different kind of thinking—unpressured."

Not yet 40, Larry is a tremendous success and has given his family everything: A luxurious, custom-built home with swimming pool and tennis courts on ten acres of rolling Maryland countryside, two vacation homes, a BMW, plus a Mitsubishi jeep. But he shows the telltale signs of severe time urgency: Short attention span, deep fatigue, the distracted air of somebody with work problems on his mind, restlessness, the sudden rush of interest when the subject turns to work, and so on.

According to Diane, Larry wasn't always like this. By nature he has a warm personality, is considerate of others, deeply centered on his family. Only six months ago, Larry had been working hard but could throw off all thoughts of work as soon as he hit the front door of his home.

"Now work is with him everywhere," says Diane, "even at home." I noticed, in fact, that their home is equipped with computer, fax machine (which goes with them to the condo or cottage), cellular phone, dictaphone, plus regular phones in every room, including the bathroom. Larry is never out of touch with his work; it's always on his mind, as the song goes. And that is why his time is never his own.

Both Larry and Diane are convinced it has to be this way. This is the price of success, a price which Diane also pays. At 39, she is bored at home. As a housewife, she says, "I'm a member of a dying breed." She would like to go back to work, but it's not possible, given Larry's work. Her time must be totally at his disposal if he is going to give all his time to work.

When I raised the subject of his time urgency with Larry, he was reluctant to explore the subject in any depth. Yet it was apparent that he found the topic painful and that he had moved to the extreme end of the time-urgency spectrum. In a six-month period, time pressures had

invaded and spread through his whole life. Like an addict, he was cling-
ing to the very treadmill that was causing his discomfort. Like an addict,
also, he tries to escape time pressures by immersing himself even further
in work.

Feeding Speed Addiction: Global-Age Time Savers

A friend of mine spent a dozen years out of the workforce while she
stayed home raising her children. When she went back to work recently
as an office manager, she was astonished. "It was like I'd been in a time
warp," Suzanne said, "and in the meantime all these wonderful machines
sprang up." She meant computers, fax machines, super multifunction
duplicators, cellular phones, calculators of immense sophistication, type-
writers that write the letters for you. When paper doesn't pour out of the
duplicators fast enough, secretaries demand a newer model right away.
Amazed by this new work culture, Suzanne dove in voraciously to learn
everything she could.

Hi-tech wonder machines seem to spawn new generations every year:
Laptop computers with more power and faster access time, fax machines
with built-in paper cutters, and cellular phones that reach incredible
distances. One company announced that it will soon put out a 25-ounce
portable phone which will fit in an overcoat pocket and permit the user
to make and receive calls from the North Pole to Antarctica. In allowing
you to always keep in touch with work, hi-tech devices also exert a subtle
pressure on people to work faster and harder. They can fuel the speed
addiction that already runs rampant in America, making it seem normal
and natural to be at work 24 hours a day.

Marty, David, Paul, and Larry are aided in their round-the-clock
efforts because of these handy little appurtenances. Larry takes his fax
machine on every vacation, even on an overnight getaway to the beach.
David has a wardrobe of computers the way other people have clothes.
Paul, in his global business, calls around the world every day: His clients
are in South America, the Pacific rim, and in downtown Manhattan;
they're all as close as his phone. Marty is in the microchip design field.
The question that needs asking is: Are they saving me time or adding to
my time pressure? The successful business people I interviewed never
ask this question. Yet every day they encounter ads such as this, for a
beeper device: "Freedom Has Its Price. $10/month. Get the freedom you
need to be more productive. Get a Bell Atlantic Pager and you can be
reached anytime. In just a matter of minutes." Advertising thus defines
our freedom for us as being captives of work.

> Ellen Goodman, syndicated columnist, writes: "I am somewhere over Connecticut on a one-hour shuttle from Boston to New York when my companion sticks his credit card into the chair before us and calls his office to find out if there are any messages. At 22,000 feet, he leaves a phone message in Boston about where to forward his phone messages in New York."

Traits of Time-Distorted People

In studying people who suffered from an extreme sense of time urgency, I gradually understood that at the heart of the problem was a misperception of time itself. In some very basic way, the present was not the present, the past was not the past, and the future was not the future. People driven by time urgency lacked any awareness of time as freely flowing in their lives. Instead, there was an underlying and painful dislocation, an inability to experience what the poet Ovid described: "Time glides by with constant movement, not unlike a stream; for neither can a stream stay its course, nor can the fleeting hour."

What's more, although they were constantly monitoring the passing of time, they were unable to see the difference between "clock time" and "lived time" in their days and hours. As the poet Henry Wadsworth Longfellow explained it, "What is time? The shadow on the dial, the striking of the clock, the running of the sand, day and night, summer and winter, months, years, centuries—these are but arbitrary and outward signs, the measures of Time, not Time itself. Time is the life of the soul."

Instead of time being the life of the soul, it became a tyrant in the daily existence of severely time-pressured people. Taking into account differences in circumstances and situation, I was able to discover in most men and women at the extreme end of the spectrum, where time urgency resembles a kind of addiction, six recognizable traits. Several of these traits show up as more intense versions of the traits I observed in those who were more mildly affected by time pressures. Not every trait appears in every person, of course.

1. Impossible Craving for a Pure Present

David is an extreme example of what most of us do initially when confronted with time pressures: We speed up our pace, trying to do everything a little bit faster so as to squeeze in more tasks, to make the absolute most of the moment we inhabit. But we set an unreal standard for ourselves. We put ourselves in a race against modern technology that is impossible to win. No human being can compute at computer speed, nor read documents as fast as they can be printed out.

David's obsession with computer time resembles a true addiction rather than an overdependence on clocks and watches that many time-driven people have. With David, the cause is not the need to monitor time but to speed it up. He is consumed by a passion to live in a pure present, one that acknowledges neither the past nor the future, because that's where the action is. To serve him, he has assembled an array of the most advanced computers available. They facilitate and exacerbate his obsession with time.

Not that David is a control freak—someone driven by an excessive urge to control people and events. He has no such need. He seeks the impossible: to control time, to master that elusive interval between what happens and our knowledge of it.

Fueled by Work Environment

David's desire is fueled by his work environment, where rewards are directly proportional to the ability to speed up time. David is indifferent to what happens. He shows no interest in events which, in themselves, are neutral, only in access to information about them. He can make money regardless of what happens. What counts is the speed at which information is communicated to him. He assigns no value to whether or not a particular event materializes. The present moment which he inhabits is not directed toward realizing a particular possibility. Any one of them will do. He has raised the adage, "knowledge is power," to an obsessive dictum in his daily work. The computer answers his need perfectly, since it provides for ever-faster access time to the present, causing the past to disappear and become irrelevant as it goes.

On the surface it appears that David's professional life is dominated by the goal of making money. But this isn't true. What drives him is the need to make the next connection, to get the "rush" of instant gratification. Money has value only as a symbol. Like his possessions, it represents an icon of success. But neither money nor possessions provide satisfaction—he may as well be a monk living an ascetic life.

As long as David continues in this addictive search for a pure present, he will not accumulate a past which might lead him to prefer one possibility rather than another. Nor will the future hold any goals for him except that of trying to devour it in converting it to the present. As a result his life has become bizarre. Dependence on the computer resembles a bonding.

Either he is an extension of his computer, or his computer of him. Whenever he must be separated from the keyboard, he is overtaken by restlessness, which stems not from fear of losing his financial success, but from his need to be constantly plugged in.

In David's life are none of the elements associated with the natural flow of time. By dismantling the past and future, he has destroyed the sense of time as that which flows in a direction. What is left to David is a present whose thinness defies imagination. But this suits his purpose. David is literally attempting to abolish time.

2. The Illusion of Controlling Time

Most people who suffer from extreme time urgency find themselves in David's predicament. They believe that speed equals control and greater speed leads to more control. Eventually they find themselves in a dilemma: They've set a pace of living that goes so far beyond their comfort zone that they feel out of control. So they develop strategies that allow them to believe they're under control—not unlike alcoholics, for example, who convince themselves they're not addicted because they never take a drink before noon, or some such stratagem.

Paul's Two Paces

Paul allows himself to put in unlimited work hours in the global economy five days a week, driving himself to such fatigue that he falls asleep as soon as he sits down to relax in the evening. But he tries to convince himself that his life is under control because he has established the inviolable rule of getting away to his country home every weekend. Thus he splits up his life into two distinct paces that he imposes on himself every week.

Larry's Interweaving Paces

Larry is similar to Paul in seeing the need to employ strategies for controlling his time. But the strategies differ and are more complex. Every day he seeks a combination of work and family time (bringing work home, doing it after the kids have gone to bed, working short hours over the weekend, and so on) which will enable him to feel he is satisfying the time demands of both his work and his home life. He weaves a spell around himself to create the illusion that his time is not out of his control.

Like a juggler, he tries to keep several balls in the air indefinitely, paying no heed to his growing fatigue and distractedness.

Marty's Escape

The most common strategy, I discovered, is the one Marty uses. He simply runs away every chance he gets, blots out all his wife's complaints. He admits that he has less than five hours of leisure time per week.

3. The Loss of Time's Pleasures

The most truly rewarding experience of human life is to sink into the moment and savor it to the full, like biting a juicy peach. It's the experience of losing awareness of time's passage while living fully in it at the moment. Those who are time-pressed lose enjoyment of time to an extreme degree; they are never there—wherever time is at the moment—but forever just ahead of themselves. The irony is that the harder you try to take hold of and control the present moment, the more it eludes your grasp. You lose a sense of duration and density, and with it the freedom and delight of time when it can be forgotten: this mysterious paradox of time's timelessness.

Melissa's Calculated Time

Melissa measures each move for its ability to facilitate her goal of becoming a law partner. So meticulously does she schedule her time that such necessities as eating, grocery shopping, laundry are subject to the one criterion of how they can least impede her progress. In her relationships, she substitutes contacts for friends, a network for a community. The only spontaneity is an occasional outburst of anger or depression, which she perceives as a threat to the facade she has carefully constructed. When a person systematically cuts out the time that must be given to relationships, like watering plants so that they will bloom into flowers, these relationships become cold, distant, and wither into nonexistence. Time given over to a single goal is transformed into dehumanized time.

4. The Dropping Out of a Usable Past

As a people we Americans have a history of disregarding the past and its precepts; it's arguably one of the qualities that accounts for our rich inventiveness. Yet the past has its valid uses. As the poet Sara Teasdale wrote, "For better than the minting / Of a gold crowned king / Is the safe memory / Of a lovely thing." People who are trapped by time urgency never enjoy memories or reflections of the past. They don't learn from the past, either. They have cut themselves off from their own history—at least in every good sense.

Melissa's Need to Prove Herself

Because Melissa's world contains no past, she constantly needs to prove herself. Although her performance is always first-rate, what she accomplished yesterday has no carryover effect today. The bottom line is the tally sheet of billable hours. In this respect she is typical of people who suffer from time distortion. Only what you do today counts. Yesterday is gone, and with it one's satisfaction in accomplishment.

Wayne's Past Pulled from under Him

In a very different way, Wayne's past has been pulled from him as if it were an old rug underfoot. He wasn't a personality drawn to a time-driven way of life, but he was thrown into it. He thought that all his past accomplishments were counting in his favor toward a better future with his company of choice, Sears, Roebuck & Co., where he had performed well for more than two decades. But the sudden and total restructuring of the company, just as happened in scores of other American corporations, told him that past performance counted little or not at all.

Stephanie: Trying to Make Up for the Past

Instead of being able to learn from the past—analyze whatever mistakes her first marriage held—and use that knowledge to make her present life better, Stephanie does the reverse. She dwells on the past in guilt and sorrow, using up precious emotional energy in a futile manner. In trying to compensate for past disappointments, she actually worsens her problem of time urgency in her current life.

5. The Shrinking of the Future

People who have fallen into a life of time urgency inevitably have a distorted perception of the future as well as the past and present. For example, the future which Melissa has created for herself—making junior partner before 30—requires her to suppress all the other futures which would ordinarily make up her life. Where there is a normal playing out of time, we would expect her life to express the fact that she is a woman, belongs to a family and a community, has friends, and, finally, enjoys a variety of personal interests and activities. Instead, her life revolves around a single goal which obliterates every other possibility. If she sought to make junior partner by 35, there would be room for other things and relationships along the way. But she has truncated the time agenda of her professional life. The resultant time distortion deprives her life of a healthy, rich three-dimensionality.

The Infinite Postponement of the Future

Melissa is acutely aware of everything she has put on hold. But she harbors the illusion that when she makes junior partner she will be able to "get out from under" the tyranny of the clock and do everything she wants to do. Her own past should tell her otherwise. Like many of her colleagues who have made it by age 30, she will find the next promotion looming before her with an equally truncated time line. Once you have proved you can succeed in a world governed by a speeded-up sense of time, others will expect, and you will expect of yourself, that you keep up the pace of performance. Melissa's future will never come because she is constantly postponing it. As it arrives, it is no different from the present. The desire for continual success is infinite and can never be satisfied.

The wives of Larry, Paul, and Marty are likewise always being forced to anticipate a future that never arrives because their husbands are obsessed with the present and its burden of work.

Wayne's Future Foreshortened

Just as the company restructuring rendered Wayne's professional past irrelevant, so did it foreshorten his long-range career plans with Sears, on which his personal future was predicated. In one sweep, the future time lines he had laid down were severed.

6. Adrift in Time: The Lost Self

As time urgency devours a person to an extreme degree, what inevitably gets lost is the self—the basic sense of who you are and where you are going in life.

The Onset of Emotional Isolation

Melissa spends little time with her family, and when she does, since both her parents are lawyers, they tend to talk law. She doesn't date men because she feels she doesn't have time, and views her colleagues as adversaries or competitors rather than potential friends. When the deprivation of leisure time to spend with family and friends becomes chronic, emotional isolation is the inevitable result.

David has no intimate friends, rarely sees his family, and invests nothing of his deep personal feelings in his business relationships. He wanders through social situations as if they were an alien landscape. The only flashes of human warmth appear in the moments when he wins a client; but that flickers out as soon as the client signs up. He operates on the conservation of energy principle, getting "hot" only for the electronic action. His life contains no spiritual center, no personality that finds expression apart from his family of computers. David has robotized himself. At the speed he travels, all connections with the natural flowing rhythms of time have long since been severed.

David's life reflects what he has done to time. He functions without any ongoing awareness of where he has come from and where he is going. Although David talks about going to California, we must not mistake this for a goal. The only difference California will make is to offer the possibility of speeding up time. There is no design to his life. He doesn't live in a present which forges a link between the past and the future. He presents an extreme, but by no means uncommon, type who suffers from Urgency Addiction.

Time Addicts Are Superstars In Our Culture

As extraordinary as his behavior seems to an observer, it seems normal to David. Nothing in his environment tells him otherwise. His colleagues, clients, and competitors see him as someone who is doing what they all do, except that he is doing it better. He is a rising superstar in the world of financial services, especially admirable because he didn't lose his nerve after the Wall Street crash of 1987.

Like many ambitious people working in high finance, David has internalized the fact that our society has long since divided time into units—each of which we have rendered productive. "Time is money" for David is not merely a maxim for achieving greater productivity and economic gains, but a perfect maxim to live by, the equivalent of a moral precept. The logic is compelling: If time is money, then surely a culture where time is measured in nanoseconds equals even more money. In financial centers across the globe, this is regarded as a truism. What goes unnoticed is that in trying to live at this electronically speeded-up pace, one loses the inner sense of time as a life-shaping process. The monetary rewards are so great that neither David nor his colleagues have time for doubts.

So, too, with Melissa. Nothing in her professional environment would serve to correct, modify, or otherwise counsel her against the time distortion by which she is living. For one thing, her colleagues are in the same boat: competing against one another for the limited number of junior partner posts. They share her assumption that making it by age 30 is the appropriate goal today. Like her, they scurry to put in a maximum number of work hours, to arrive in early morning, to land new clients, and to increase the hours billed to current clients. In her peers, she sees herself mirrored.

Melissa's superiors in the firm further reinforce her sense of time urgency. They praise and reward her for totaling up the billable hours at a fast rate. She has never heard her boss say, "Slow down a bit, Melissa," or "No need to hurry." Moreover, when she steps outside the doors of her own law firm, she finds the same imperatives in the broader professional and corporate climate where she does her legal work. Her daily schedule runs among successful executives who respond aggressively to a competitive world where time urgency seems normal, indeed even becomes a status symbol: The more rushed you are, the more important you must be.

The make-it-by-30 syndrome is taken for granted; those who haven't made it by then get relegated to the slow track (which is for boring losers). The glamour look goes with speed. Speed and time awareness are such valued commodities that they rate high on the list of rules for professional etiquette. Thus Melissa faces extraordinary time pressures both within and outside the firm vis à vis her clients. The firm measures Melissa's performance by the number of hours she bills clients, for this is the bottom line relating to the firm's profits. But the reverse is true for clients: They seek the maximum amount of legal work accomplished for the minimum number of hours billed. Melissa's most important task is to satisfy both sides while continuing to impress the senior partners favorably with the quality of her legal expertise so as to win a partnership.

Like many others, Melissa is thus caught in a time trap that is both internal and external. That is why she cannot rid herself of her blind spot regarding time. Her external environment validates the distorted sense of time that rules her life; it mirrors her psychological state, reinforcing and validating it rather than offering a contrasting view.

There's a Way to Get Free of Time Distortion

Nobody is immune to time pressure in America today. Many people suffer from a sense of time urgency so severe that it actually distorts their perception of time. But the fact that this problem is widespread does not mean it is insoluble. Quite the opposite is true. There is a way to get free of the weight of time pressure. You can be among those who leave this burden behind and move forward to a better life.

4

THE URGENCY INDEX
Four Self-Tests: Identifying Time Distortion

Now here, you see, it takes all the running you can do,

to keep in the same place.

If you want to get somewhere else,

you must run at least twice as fast as that!

—LEWIS CARROLL, *THROUGH THE LOOKING GLASS*

n the midst of running a time treadmill, it can be very difficult to see clearly what is happening to us. There is the sense that time is out of our control, that we're not doing well, things aren't right somehow. We may experience confusion, discouragement, fatigue, and irritability and yet not know how to make ourselves feel better. We may appreciate the obvious irony that we don't have time to figure out how to get out of the time trap. We just keep running the treadmill, getting ourselves more and more into a rut.

We may succeed at carrying on our usual responsibilities at home or work while feeling emotionally battered by every wind that blows our way. We may get stuck in our schedule, struggling repeatedly with the daily round of demands, dropping into bed exhausted every night, planning only how to make it through the next day rather than how to solve the problem.

There is a way out. If we can step outside the harrying routine just long enough to get the problem clarified, we can start feeling better. We can then see that the process of getting freed from time pressures consists of a series of decisions, followed by emotional and mental changes, concluding with new behaviors and actions. People who have felt they were forced onto a grueling treadmill finally begin to touch firm ground when they can observe their situations with objectivity. With insight, it is possible to move beyond the crisis situation and then go vigorously ahead.

The first step toward freedom is to take the measure of the problem. What follows is a series of four self-tests. They will help you pinpoint the areas in your life, as well as the attitudes, assumptions, and behaviors, that are the sources of your time urgency.

TEST 1: *Your Career.* Answer yes or no to each question below in the space provided at the right:

1. Do you put in 50 hours or more on the job most weeks? _____

2. If a meeting is cancelled, do you regard this as "found time" for more work? _____

3. Do you usually conduct business on your lunch hour? _____

4. Are you reluctant to take a vacation? _____

5. Do you attend 3 or more meetings most workdays? _____

6. Do you set up 2 or 3 power breakfasts a week? _____

7. Are you available to your boss 7 days a week? _____

8. Do you hate to take time off when you're sick? _____

9. At business meetings, do you race to the phone during breaks to call the office? _____

10. Does your cellular phone go everywhere with you? _____

11. Can your secretary always reach you? _____

12. Do you feel indispensable at work? _____

13. Do you use your car for doing business (via phone, laptop computer, or tape recorder)? _____

14. Is your schedule so full that your secretary constantly has to juggle appointments? _____

15. Is your job always on your mind? _____

16. Do you have several techniques for getting rid of people when their time is up? _____

17. Do you relate to staff mainly by giving orders? _____

18. Do you snap at staff members if they're slow? _____

19. Is it important for you to "make it" as young as possible? _____

20. Do you often compare your career status to that of others your own age or younger? _____

21. Do you sometimes feel the company you work for has stolen the best years of your life? _____

22. Is it impossible to shorten your work hours? _____

23. Does the thought of time off make you uneasy? _____

24. Do you find it hard to concentrate on anything besides work? _____

SCORE: _____ yes _____ no

TEST 2: *Your Relationships.* Answer true or false to each question below:

1. At social gatherings, my mind often darts ahead to the next day's work schedule. _____

2. I'm often restless at family get-togethers. _____

3. Most of my social contacts relate to my work. _____

4. I feel truly comfortable only at work. _____

5. I'm glad when the weekend is over. _____

6. I measure my worth by how much I accomplish each day. _____

7. My tendency is to time my leisure activities. _____

8. I panic if friends drop in unexpectedly. _____

9. I get my physical exercise through competitive sports and/or fitness routines in which I push myself to the limit. _____

10. If I weren't busy all the time, I'd go crazy. _____

11. I often have to "make a date" to spend time with my family. _____

12. My most rewarding relationships are with business associates. _____

13. It's hard to keep in touch with old friends. _____

14. I would cut back the fast pace I'm on if I weren't having fun. _____

15. None of my friends knows me as I really am. _____

SCORE: _____ true _____ false

TEST 3: *Getting from Here to There.* Answer yes or no to each question below:

1. Does a slow elevator annoy you? _____

2. Do you anticipate a "worst possible scenario" when making travel plans? _____

3. If the car ahead of you doesn't move when the light turns green, do you honk? _____

4. When driving, do you exceed the speed limit to avoid being late? _____

5. Do you arrive early to most appointments? _____

6. In line at the bank or supermarket, do you watch other lines to see if yours is the fastest? _____

7. Do you second-guess the taxi driver's route? _____

8. When planning transportation, do you factor in traffic tie-ups and unforeseen delays? _____

9. Do you routinely recheck train and plane schedules as well as maps? _____

10. When driving, do you route yourself to avoid traffic lights? _____

11. If someone ahead of you at the checkout counter fumbles with a checkbook, do you grumble? _____

12. If possible, do you bypass people on the escalator? _____

SCORE: _____ yes _____ no

TEST 4: *Your Sense of Self:* Answer true or false to each of the questions below:

1. I have no time for myself. _____

2. I frequently tell myself that as soon as I finish the project I'm working on, I'll do what I really want to do. _____

3. I seldom daydream anymore. _____

4. I've begun feeling that time is passing me by. _____

5. I rarely think about the meaning of life. _____

6. I haven't set spiritual goals for my life.   ____

7. I never relax outdoors just to watch what's going on.   ____

8. I rarely do anything on impulse, just for the fun of it.   ____

9. Sometimes I promise myself that I'll spend a few weeks
having a real vacation.   ____

10. I seldom ask myself if I'm happy.   ____

11. I often feel sleep-deprived.   ____

12. If I had the time, I would read more books.   ____

SCORE: _____ true _____ false

Scoring Key for Self-Tests

Test 1. Your Career. Count the number of times you answered yes.

0 to 8:   You have nothing to worry about. You are clearly a busy professional who is handling your workload intelligently.

9 to 14:   There is reason to believe that the line between being busy and being driven by time pressure has gotten blurred in your worklife.

15 to 24:   You are suffering from an excessive sense of time urgency on the job. The more times you answered yes, the greater the pressure you feel.

Test 2. Your Relationships. Count the number of times you answered true.

0 to 4:   The problem of time urgency has not invaded your personal life and social relationships.

5 to 9:   Time pressures have entered your private life to a significant degree.

10 to 15:   Your meaningful relationships with other people are seriously threatened. The balance in your life is upset.

Test 3. Getting from Here to There. Tally up the number of yes answers.

0 to 4:   Relax! You're simply experiencing the normal frustrations of everyday transportation. They're unavoidable.

5 to 8:   You are definitely focusing your sense of time urgency on transportation and logistics issues.

9 to 12:   You are masking your problem with time urgency behind transportation worries.

Test 4. Your Sense of Self. Add up the number of times you answered true.

1 to 3:   You don't give the time to yourself which you deserve.

4 to 8:   Your excessive sense of time urgency has caused damage to your inner self. The more times you answered true, the deeper the loss and deprivation to yourself.

9 to 12:   In succumbing to feelings of time pressure, you have taken away necessary and precious time from yourself. To deprive yourself to this extent is self-destructive.

Now Take a Look at Yourself

Consider all your answers. Examine them carefully, one at a time, and each in relation to the others. It's as if you were looking at your face in a mirror. How you spend your time eventually makes you the person you are. Look at the way time plays out in your life, and see the person you've become. It is important that you look at yourself thoughtfully, through an undistorted lens, in order to get a true picture. As you take steps to free up the time of your life—which you will learn how to do in the following chapters—this picture of yourself will serve as the starting point to which you can return again and again to mark your progress.

Trace Your Personal Pattern

You need to see exactly the pattern that time distortion takes in your life. Has it permeated every aspect, or only part of it? How intense is your feeling of time urgency? To what extent have you turned over your time to others? How deep is your sense of a lost self? If you find that the major area in which you suffer time urgency is your career, it is very understandable. You can, after all, point to the not-so-hidden messages of our society, such as "60-hour weeks are expected if you want to get ahead." But messages from the corporate culture are not good enough principles on which to live your life.

It's Time to Make Changes

You've already taken two important steps in the right direction. First, you've "stolen" enough time from your very busy life to pay attention to

Transportation Urgency

Why does time urgency so often express itself as worry and frustration about transportation? The best answer I found is that so much of every busy person's life is taken up by getting from here to there, and time is often of the essence. A recent study by the Census Bureau showed that there has been a tremendous increase in travel by Americans. The breakdown goes like this: 30.1 percent of miles traveled were getting to or from work; 13.4 percent were for shopping and 15.5 percent were for other personal business; 13.3 percent were for social and recreational activities; 1 percent was for leisure; and 2.1 percent were for vacations.

In passenger miles, domestic airline travel has soared from 119 billion in 1970 to 341 billion in 1987, while the number of cars has increased far out of proportion to miles of roads in the United States. In 1970 there were 61 yards of road per vehicle, but by 1986 the space shrank to only 39 yards per vehicle. The number of miles driven has likewise increased by an incredible amount. In 1970 vehicle miles traveled in the United States were roughly the equivalent of two million round-trips to the moon. Now cars are driven about three million round-trips annually.

Longer commutes to work, added to ever-denser traffic and everlonger delays, total up to significant and widespread transportation urgency. Forecasts are that in the next 10 to 15 years, vehicle miles traveled will jump an additional 25 to 40 percent. The response of making the inside of cars "comfort cocoons" is a mixed blessing: fax machines, laptop computers, and cellular phones for doing business can actually increase time pressure rather than reduce it.

a serious problem. This implies a healthy concern for yourself, an act of self-esteem which is crucial to your climbing out of the time trap which I call Urgency Addiction. Second, you've taken this simple set of tests which have provided you with an awareness of the extent of your problem. Good for you. Now you are ready to construct your road map to freedom. You can discover a more vital, exhilarating sense of time, one which leads to happiness. You don't need to worry that you will have to sacrifice your success. Quite the reverse is true.

What's Normal and Natural Time?

Urgency Addiction occurs when you wake up one morning and realize you've slipped from being merely very busy to being driven by time. It's always on your mind. Soon this leads to a panicky sense that your life is out of control. An early tendency is to develop certain coping skills which enable you to mask it from your work colleagues. You divide time into units; chop these units into smaller and smaller "bytes" in order to make them more productive. You live by the clock and step up the pace of your daily activities. You drop from your life whatever can be let go—often those things which are most essential to a satisfying life. Above all, you feel driven by time.

As a result, you go against the natural rhythms that belong to an unfolding process, and you are left with a distorted sense of time. The problem arises surreptitiously because we usually "look through" time, barely noticing its existence. As St. Augustine observed back in the Middle Ages, we know what time is until someone asks us to explain it. Time is as difficult to pin down as the air we breathe, yet it is just as real. Like life, time is always "on the move." In fact, time appears to us as the very form of life itself. Our awareness of being alive is inseparable from our sense of a past and a future linking to form the present moment.

We live many roles simultaneously—for example, that of daughter, spouse, mother, sister, friend, colleague, artist, physician, citizen, community activist, and so on. Each role is like a strand which weaves itself in and out of every other role. They make up the time lines of a life; woven together they create the rich tapestry we call our very selves.

There is a time that naturally belongs to each of these strands, providing the myriad textures and rhythms of our experience. The distortion of time, which I call Urgency Addiction, arises as a disruption in the time lines that make up our lives. At the least, an imbalance occurs. At its most severe, the very self is plunged onto a destructive course. It's not simply the attempt to fly too fast and too high that results in self-destruction. It's losing a sense of the inner synchronization of self with the time of one's life. What starts out as a loss of balance can lead to a loss of self.

As you read from chapter to chapter, go at the pace that seems right for you. Some aspects of the program will seem more pertinent to you than others. Give as much or as little time to each phase of the program as you feel is needed. Be assured of this. Although it will be difficult at first to restore and rebalance your time, the effort will be worth it. In transforming the time of your life, you will regain your life and attain a new, deeper sense of yourself.

Knowledge is power. *Understanding* is the path to freedom. In the next chapter, I'll recount for you the journey I took to discover how Urgency Addiction became a major force in American life today.

5

IT'S NOT A PERSONALITY PROBLEM: HOW TIME PRESSURES TOOK US OVER

Do not squander Time, for that's the Stuff Life is made of.

—BENJAMIN FRANKLIN

Time urgency lies buried in the bones of our collective past. It is deeply embedded in the American character. I suspected from the start that the roots of this pervasive time pressure were to be found in our history as a people. The more I delved, the further I was drawn into our American past. Finally, I found myself in the Puritan culture of early Boston, where the famous divine, Cotton Mather, exemplified the hard-working, time-driven prototypical American of the seventeenth century.

Cotton Mather: Hurrying for Salvation

Cotton Mather's life could rival the busiest American's today. He married three times, fathered 15 children, wrote 450 books, headed a church, gave thousands of sermons, chaired numerous conferences, visited the sick and the poor, and all the while chided himself for laziness. Throughout his life of prodigious accomplishment, he exhibited the telltale signs of time urgency typical of present-day Americans: Obsessive diary keeping, which catalogued his daily actions; chronic list making; an ever-present awareness of time passing and the need to account for it; and a relentless scrutiny of his own use of time.

Motivated by the desire for heavenly gain as well as worldly renown, in his diary Cotton Mather frequently recorded his urgent desire to fill up productively "the little Parcels, Fragments, and Intervals of Time" in which most people let their minds "lie like the Field of the Sluggard, overgrown with Weeds." He wanted his time to be "so well-husbanded"

61

that "at all Places of Diversion, I would be at my spiritual Alchemy," working toward the goal of eternal salvation. He never ceased monitoring himself, having an insatiable need to fill up every time fragment.

In his diary he quizzed himself: "When I am abroad among my Neighbors, would it be more pleasing unto my glorious Lord, that I should be in my Study at this Time? If I find myself in a Temper and Vigour to be carrying on greater services in my Study, I would break off the most agreeable Conversation, and fly thither, with a Zeal of redeeming the Time, upon me." Like the contemporary time-driven American, he felt guilty enjoying himself at leisure with friends.

For Cotton Mather, as for many of us today, time was not incidental, but a central feature of his life. We would call him a zealot, except that he sounds so much like us. In 1706, he headed the diary beginning his 44th year: "How My Time Is Taken Up," then began woefully, "Alas, for a very great Part of my Time, I am dead. It is consumed in Sleep. Thro' my Slothfulness, I rise not until seven or eight a Clock." He then lists his 31 daily activities, showing how much time is allotted to each task, concerned not only to track his hours but to spur himself on to more work.

Cotton nagged his Boston Church congregation to spend its time better, publishing a pamphlet which included proposals "to prevent that great Mischief, the Loss of Time; and employ the Talent of Time so watchfully and fruitfully that a good account may at least be given of it."

Although Cotton strutted about with plenty of worldly ambition, his time urgency was largely fueled by the religious force of Puritanism. He felt driven to perform to a high moral standard as proof that he ranked among God's elect. As a man past 60, he resolved in his diary to "make it a daily Petition to Him: Lord, make me a wise Redeemer of the little Time that remains unto me!"

Benjamin Franklin: Time Is Money

In the generation following Cotton Mather, Benjamin Franklin was an exemplary time-driven American of the eighteenth century. He also had a life of outstanding accomplishment, noted as a man of affairs, diplomat, author, and scientist. Known also for his recognition of time's importance, he admired Cotton Mather's zeal for filling up every segment of time productively, and consciously tried to emulate him.

Ben Franklin, like many others from colonial times, was a journal keeper, an inveterate list maker and scheduler, a deviser of plans, determined not to waste a minute. Echoing Mather, he once wrote, "How much more than is necessary do we spend in Sleep! forgetting that there will be sleeping enough in the Grave."

But there was an important shift. The reason for making every minute count changed. Franklin's time urgency was fueled more by secular than religious motives. He formulated the equation that time equals money, exhorting his fellow Americans to use time well, not so much to gain entrance to the heavenly kingdom, but to achieve earthly success. Making time productive could lead you to wealth. Thus the concern with time is deeply embedded in our national character, not only as a moral imperative, but as a sure path to wealth and success.

Franklin wrote to a friend who asked for advice, "Remember that *TIME* is Money. He that can earn Ten Shillings a Day by his Labour, and goes abroad, or sits idle one half of that Day, tho' he spends but Sixpence during his Diversion or Idleness, ought not to reckon That the only Expence. He was really spent or rather thrown away Five Shillings besides."

His advice was always pithy: "In short, the Way to Wealth, if you desire it, is as plain as the Way to Market. Waste neither Time nor Money, but make the best Use of both."

Like many of us Americans dependent on our Filofaxes, Franklin always carried his little book with him. He kept track of his days on an hourly basis, made goals for them, and then assessed his achievements at the end of the day. Recognizing that some people might criticize his advice to be always working at maximum capacity, he gave this answer:

"Methinks I hear some of you say, Must a Man afford himself no Leisure? I will tell thee, my Friend, what Poor Richard says. Employ thy Time well if thou meanest to gain Leisure; and since thou art not sure of a Minute, throw not away an Hour. Leisure is Time for doing something useful; this Leisure the diligent Man will obtain, but the lazy Man never."

Poor Richard's Sayings

- If Time be of all Things the most precious, wasting Time must be the greatest Prodigality, since Lost Time is never found again.
- And what we call Time enough, always proves little enough.
- He that riseth late, must trot all Day, and shall scarce overtake his Business at Night.
- Early to Bed, and early to rise, makes a Man healthy, wealthy and wise.
- Work while it is called To-day, for you know not how much you may be hindered To-morrow.
- One To-day is worth two To-morrows.
- Have you somewhat to do To-morrow, do it To-day.

The Nineteenth Century: From Natural Time to Clock Time

Until the middle of the nineteenth century, most Americans lived on farms, their days governed by natural time. Work, recreation, eating, exercise, traveling, and socializing were all governed and regulated according to the natural course of the days and seasons. Sunrise, sunset, rain, snow, heat, cold, fall, winter, spring, and summer: These were the natural time segments by which people organized their lives. But with the move to the fast-growing cities and the factories that reflected the emerging industrialization, nature's time gave way to clock time. The mechanical clock ticking rather than the sun traversing the meridian began to rule many people's lives as never before.

At first, the shift of workplace from farm to factory or shop in town was still guided by the natural limitation of the sun and moon: Candlelight did not encourage a lengthened workday. Moreover, workers could control the pace and rhythm of their effort, much as they had in the fields and barns. But radical changes were precipitated by the invention of a single American genius. Thereafter, timekeeping in America would never be the same, and time urgency would take on new dimensions.

Thomas Edison's Light Bulb Extended the Day

In 1879, when Thomas Edison invented the first commercially practical incandescent lamp with a carbon filament, he also developed a complete electrical distribution system for light and power, including generators, motors, light sockets with the Edison base, junction boxes, safety fuses, underground conductors, and other devices. The Pearl Street plant in New York City constructed in 1881–82 was the first central, electric-light power plant in the world. Workers would no longer be dependent upon the light of the sun. The stage was set to start the workday before sunup and to extend it beyond sundown.

Ford's Assembly Line Revolutionized Work Time

In the same year that Edison invented the light bulb, Henry Ford was a 16-year-old boy who left his father's Michigan farm to work as an apprentice in a Detroit machine shop. In 1892 he completed the invention of his first car, and in 1899, near the dawn of the twentieth century, he launched the Detroit Automobile Company. By 1907 he controlled his own Ford Motor Company.

When Ford put a highly mechanized assembly line into his Highland Park auto factory, he radically changed the lives of American workers. The conveyor belt, the traveling platform, the overhead rails, and material conveyors created an entirely new way of working. The workers no longer had the reins of the plowhorse in their own hands, walking their own pace under the sun. Instead of being drivers, they were being driven. Now lined up in front of a moving belt, they were constrained to work at a common pace dictated by the moving belt, or more precisely, by the boss who controlled the belt's speed. The time it took to do the work was dictated by an outside force. Time pressure took on new meaning.

As Shoshana Zuboff comments in her recent book, *In the Age of the Smart Machine* (Basic Books, 1988), "The history of work has been, in part, the history of the worker's body. Production depended on what the body could accomplish with strength and skill." With earlier production methods, "the supervisor could partially control output by giving directions, but with Henry Ford, the control became absolute. The moving belt set the pace. The worker became a *reactor*, not an *actor*. Time moved absolutely out of his control."

Meanwhile, the conveyor belt and assembly line helped propel Ford upwards to become the brilliant star of mass production. By cutting the costs of production, and by gaining control of raw materials and the means of distribution as well, he outdistanced every competitor and landed on top as the leading producer of automobiles in the world. More than 15 million Model T Fords were sold between 1908 and 1928. The machine age was entrenched in America, and the groundwork was laid for a vastly more widespread time pressure applied to workers.

The slogan which Benjamin Franklin had urged upon the farmers and merchants of his day was "Haste makes Waste." But the new slogan sparked by the assembly lines became "Speed equals Productivity which increases Profit." Here lay a revolutionary change. The Franklin dictum, "Time is Money," had acquired a new meaning: The worker's time equaled the owner's profit.

The assembly line moved us further away from natural time as more and more Americans, forsaking rural farms for city factories, got accustomed to living by the mechanical ticking of the clock rather than the rhythms of the sun and seasons. The direct touch and bond with nature were weakened. Also weakened was the power that men and women exercised over their worktime. Workers lost control over the number of hours spent at work daily, but even more important, they lost autonomy over the *pace* at which they exerted themselves minute by minute, day by day, in the factory assembly lines.

Taylor and Gilbreth: Taking Over Workers' Time

When the concept of scientific management came along in the early twentieth century, it fit hand in glove with the goals of the developing machine age. The theory of scientific management held that productivity could be greatly increased by examining and analyzing, then streamlining and reorganizing every operation within factory walls. The time study was the favored method, and its chief exponent was Frederick Taylor (1856–1915), who came to be loved by owners and hated by workers, and whose work became *Principles of Scientific Management* (1911). Later on, Frank Gilbreth (1868–1924) gained prominence as a time-and-motion expert, and put his research into *Applied Motion Study* (1917).

Between the two of them, Taylor and Gilbreth (equipped with time sheets and stopwatches) observed workers on the job and sought to isolate and identify every separate action in order to codify a rational process in which the most efficient series of actions could be mandated while all wasted effort was eliminated. As Shoshana Zuboff reports, "Taylorism explicitly treats the worker's body in its two dimensions— as a source of effort and as a source of skill." She comments, "The goal was to slice to the core of an action, preserving what was necessary and discarding the rest." This observation by experts "made it possible to translate actions into units of time and reconstruct them more efficiently."

Of course, as soon as the experts had extracted the information about how workers performed, the workers lost a crucial authority over themselves. In the transfer of knowledge from the workers to the owners, there was also a transfer of power. The workers ceded their know-how to others

---

How Fast to Work?

"A machinist gained prominence when he debated Taylor in 1914 and remarked, 'We don't want to work as fast as we are able to. We want to work as fast as we think it's comfortable for us to work. We haven't come into existence for the purpose of seeing how great a task we can perform through a lifetime. We are trying to regulate our work so as to make it auxiliary to our lives.'"

—Shoshana Zuboff
In the Age of the Smart Machine

who would then tell them how to use that know-how. As Zuboff points out, "The data from the time-motion study sheets became the possession of management and helped to fuel an explosion in the ranks of those who would measure, analyze, plan, report, issue orders, and monitor the various aspects of the production process." Once the control of their own time, their own pace, was gone, workers would discover that they had also lost much of their satisfaction and pride in accomplishment.

When these revolutionary changes occurred—the mechanized assembly line and the time-and-motion approach to management—the twentieth century was still in its infancy. The pace of American worklife was still at a trot compared to the runaway speed that was about to get going. Another revolution had its start when American businesspeople realized that the wedding of the machine to the principles of scientific management could ultimately increase profits far beyond anything the body of man could ever attempt. The dream machine arrived in the shape of a computer.

The Computerization of Time-Driven America

World War II had hardly ended when a new dawn of unimagined speed arose with the invention of the computer. In the race with time, the computer took us light-years ahead, so much that as the twentieth century advanced, our society became by and large totally dissociated from the rhythms of natural time. Our world as it approaches the twenty-first century is driven by the time patterns of the computer.

The computer radically changed the whole work world. In fact, the burgeoning technology of the twentieth century has sparked the eruption of one revolution after another. This daring electronic invention, able to compute faster than the minds of most men can imagine, and with new generations of ever more powerful machines getting hatched at dizzying speed, now dominates our economic life.

A new pace, a new standard of measuring the passage of time, has altered the fabric and rhythm of our society so dramatically that we are now two dimensions removed from our natural sense of time. Men and women approach the twenty-first century workplace with the computer as the dominant "model" for time, replacing traditional clocks. It's nanoseconds and milliseconds instead of minutes and seconds. In long-range terms, corporations plan their futures according to incredibly foreshortened time lines.

Inventing the Speed Machine

In 1930 Vannevar Bush, an American scientist, built a mechanically operated device called a *differential analyzer,* which was the first general-purpose analog computer. The first information-processing digital computer built was the Automatic Sequence Controlled Calculator, or Mark I computer, designed by American engineer Howard Aiken and completed in 1944. The Electronic Numerical Integrator and Computer (ENIAC) was put into operation in 1946; it was the first electronic digital computer. Norbert Wiener of the Massachusetts Institute of Technology, known for his theory of cybernetics, contributed to the development of electronic computers.

The computer is the logical extension of the clock. Typical computer clock rates range from several million cycles per second to several hundred million, with some of the fastest computers having clock rates of about a billion cycles per second. Operating at these speeds, digital computers are capable of performing thousands to millions of arithmetic operations per second, thus permitting the rapid solution of problems so long that they would be impossible for a human being to solve by hand. Computer scientists dream of someday calculating in femtoseconds, doing a million billion calculations per second.

The time pressure on us as a society derives from the sheer, ever-increasing pace and volume of information which spews out of the screens and printers and duplicators all across America. We feel it is incumbent upon us to *act on it.* Something, in short, has to be done with and about all this data. As a significant response, we have created an "infinite" workweek: the 24-hour day and the 7-day week. Gone forever are regular hours and set schedules. Our hi-tech economy whirls around the globe, operating at breakneck speed night and day. Millions of American workers (estimates vary from 10 to 20 million) have night shifts or rotating shifts on a permanent basis. As the "family" of computers, ranging from the giant supercomputers to the tiny laptops, becomes relatively more powerful and less expensive, the inevitable trickle-down effect is to drive our time-based society at an ever accelerating pace.

Nine Amazing Computer Facts

The core of computer-based technology is the silicon-integrated circuit, or "chip." The equivalent of hundreds of thousands of transistors can be built on a silicon chip measuring no more than a fraction of an inch. The chip's progress through the last 40 years is an irresistible headlong movement of increasing speed and accuracy combined with decreasing size and cost. Consider these facts:

1. A computer computation that would have cost about $30,000 in 1950 now costs one dollar.
2. Between 1958 and 1980, the amount of time needed for one electronic operation fell by a factor of 80 million.
3. Businesses face the task of handling 400 billion computer-generated documents annually, a number increasing at a yearly rate of 72 billion.
4. Modems, devices that allow two or more computers to share information over regular telephone lines, are speeding up. The standard office modem able to transfer 1,200 or 2,400 bits of information a second will soon leap to 9,600 bits a second, using data compression, which squeezes out the "white space" between chunks of data.
5. In February 1989, Texas Instruments announced that it had developed a superfast memory chip that can hold one million bits of information. This device, called a static random access memory chip (SRAM), retrieves a bit of information in just 8-billionths of a second, compared to about 20-billionths of a second for existing commercially available SRAMs.
6. In April 1989, HNSX Supercomputers, Inc., a joint venture of Honeywell, Inc. and Japan's NEC Corporation, unveiled the world's fastest supercomputer, which it said was up to 8 times more powerful than any current model, with a clock speed of under 3 nanoseconds—or 3-billionths of a second—and a memory capability of up to 2 million bytes.
7. In June 1990, Tandy Corporation introduced its latest laptop, a 6.7-pound portable with a full keyboard and a removable 20-megabyte hard disk. When workers have to go on the road, they can simply plug in their own hard disks, thus bringing along the entire contents of their desktop machines.

8. In June 1990, Hitachi, Ltd. of Japan announced a working prototype of a 64-megabit memory chip—one that can store more than 64 million bits of information and could pave the way for desktop supercomputers. A decade ago, the 64-kilobit chip, able to store about 64,000 bits of information, was the cutting edge of memory technology. The 1-megabit chip is now standard, although the 16-megabit generation is on its way.

9. In 1992, Thinking Machines Corporation is scheduled to deliver the first prototype of its teraflop supercomputers. Now supercomputer speed is measured by gigaflop—a billion operations per second. The teraflop, 1,000 times faster, represents a trillion operations.

Workstations as Time-Control Devices

The introduction of computers to the offices of America on a grand scale has transformed the way we spend our time within corporate walls. One analyst estimated that in 1990, 50 million American office workers spent a significant part of their workday interacting with a computer terminal of some sort, up from 10 million in 1980. As corporate leaders have used scientific management principles to structure computer work, an office assembly line has formed. The workstation has become the office equivalent of the factory worker's position in front of the moving belt.

The workstation, as a perfectly self-contained unit for a single worker, is designed for efficiency and maximum productivity, with every resource needed to do the job enclosed within an individual's cubicle. The emphasis shifts from interpersonal communication to interfacing with a video display terminal (VDT); all that one must do is to manipulate data presented in electronic symbols on a screen. Theoretically, the "white space" of irrelevant actions and communication is removed. The more scientifically the system is designed, the less reason there is for a clerk ever to get up from the workstation chair. From management's point of view, the workstation has removed all obstacles to continuous production. A supervisor monitors productivity simply by dipping into the computer. Ideally, each workstation can be measured in units of productive time, which can be converted to a dollar figure.

But the benefits to employers offer little satisfaction to employees inhabiting these cubicles. Just as factory workers assigned to the assembly line and subjected to Taylorism found the pace of their efforts as well as control of their know-how transferred to management, so, too, have office workers met with a similar fate.

Their time is no longer under their control. Despite the relative mindlessness of the data entry process, workers need to be consciously and constantly engaged with the VDT. There is now no escape. Partitions between each workstation provide isolation, but not privacy. Both dignity and mental ease are diminished. The release from manual labor which the computer affords has instead served to step up productivity demands in such a way that, once again, the *pace*—the rhythm of how one spends one's time on the job—has been taken out of the worker's hands. If you can't set a pace that feels right to you, then your time is taken away from you in a radical new way. Punching a clock at beginning and end of day is a minimal control compared to the ongoing total absorption of your attention. Inhabiting a workstation, a worker is reduced to a tiny time unit.

The Assembly Line on Japanese Time

Earlier in this chapter we encountered the factory assembly line at Henry Ford's auto factory as the twentieth century was beginning. It's worth noting that nothing essential has changed except the cast of characters. Some of our most up-to-date auto assembly plants are now run by the Japanese, who are taking over American auto plants at a brisk clip.

When a General Motors plant closed in Fremont, California, New United Motor Manufacturing, Inc. (NUMMI) took it over as a joint venture between Toyota and General Motors. This NUMMI plant has an assembly line with a conveyor that extends a mile and an eighth. Every day 850 cars are built along this line, with a car exiting every 60 seconds. Each workstation is marked by yellow lines on either side.

Above the workers, within easy reach, is a cord to pull if a worker gets in trouble and can't keep up the pace. When the cord is pulled, a light flashes, music starts to play, and the team leader comes running to help.

This NUMMI plant operates at maximum efficiency. Every operation is timed repeatedly to find out if a few seconds could be shaved off by simplifying an action. If the team falls even a minute or two behind schedule, the supervisor announces it. When we in America invented time-and-motion efficiency, we called it Taylorism. The Japanese have their word too: *kaizan*. On TV's *48 Hours*, a sequence was filmed at NUMMI, and part of the dialogue went like this:

Interviewer: What happens when you get behind?

Worker: I just work faster. If I can't, I call a team leader to help me out.

Interviewer: What's that called, when you get behind?

Worker: "In the hole."

Interviewer: That means you go past the yellow line?

Worker: That means, yeah, you're going down for the count. You can't do it anymore, you're out of control.

Interviewer: Critics say NUMMI manages by stress, always scrutinizing, always pressing the assembly line to the limit.

Worker: I think it's just the minute-by-minute doing your job, always working at somebody else's pace. You can't do the job any other way than the way it's supposed to be done because that's the most efficient way to do it. *Kaizan*-ing is supposed to be creative, but I mean, how many times can you sit there and *kaizan* a job after you've done it for four and a half years?

Second Worker: Things have changed so much from General Motors to NUMMI. I mean, the things that we wouldn't tolerate, we have to tolerate here because of the market that we have. So I think a lot of people walk on eggs, you know, and maybe that's good. It keeps them alert. Because I watched General Motors go right down the tubes, you know, and I'm not going to let it happen again.

First Worker: Just keep me in a job and I'll do it the way you want me to do it. (Excerpted from "Fast Times," Transcript of March 8, 1990, show of CBS-TV's *48 Hours.*)

Global Time Rushes Headlong into the Future

The computerization of work in America has acquired additional power and speed by being wedded to the scientific management principles that we can trace to the early twentieth century. But even more fundamental to the force and vigor—the mightiness—of our ever accelerating pace is the American notion of time as units for moral and monetary productivity. Cotton Mather and Benjamin Franklin led the way as our forebears. If we visualize time as tiny slots capable of almost infinite filling up, it's clear that such a picture can both energize us and make us feel tremendously pressured. This phenomenon of being time driven permeates all phases of American worklife: Whether we *see* it or not, we most certainly *feel* it.

   The effects of these conditions as they are happening in America have their worldwide reverberations, too. They are manifested in the rapidly advancing move toward a global economy. As authors John Naisbitt and Patricia Aburdene point out in their recent book, *Megatrends 2000* (William Morrow, 1990), "We are in an unprecedented period of accelerated change, perhaps the most breathtaking of which is the swiftness of our rush to all the world's becoming a single economy." This awareness of a sudden and remarkable opening up of grandiose spaces, which symbolize the appearance of vastly fertile markets, makes people in business feel called upon to rush faster than ever. Every new opportunity, it seems, must be found and seized.

Communicating at the Speed of Light

The advancing global economy is fueled by the speed-up of world telecommunications. As authors Naisbitt and Aburdene point out, "We are moving toward the capability to communicate anything to anyone, anywhere, by any form—voice, data, text, or image—at the speed of light."

The medium for this transformation is the fiber-optic cable, a tremendous technological leap beyond copper wires; a single fiber-optic cable can carry more than 8,000 conversations, compared with 48 for a copper wire. On December 14, 1988, the first fiber-optic telephone cable went into service across the Atlantic. This new cable can carry 40,000 calls simultaneously, tripling the volume of the three existing copper cables plus satellites. Before the year 2000, a single optic fiber will be able to transmit 10 million conversations at the same time compared with only 3,000 in 1988.

What Price Speed?

Economic and communications globalization dramatically affects the sense of time we live by. The speed-up of clock time to the rhythms of computer time, with the reverberating beat of global time always subliminally in our consciousness, has changed our very existence. We have stepped up the pace so much that our sense of living time according to the rhythms of nature has virtually been destroyed. Our psyches experience this as an increase in time pressure.

We've sacrificed intimacy with a crucial aspect of ourselves. We're part nature, part culture, and we need to satisfy both in order to fulfill ourselves as human beings. As nature's time has shrunk, clock time has overtaken our lives and set a pace faster than anything known in the history of humanity. Distortion results when we lose our inner sense of synchronization with natural rhythms.

The time urgency that we feel as individuals is lodged in our national character as Americans, and in the global explosion of high technology. You can't change the world, but you can change yourself. By understanding the situation, you can find the way to get free of the time pressures which are limiting your enjoyment of life. You are ready to turn to yourself and begin a program for becoming a time-integrated person. You are about to learn how to gain back dominion of your time.

Overcoming
Urgency Addiction
in Your Personal Life

6

THE TURNING POINT: DECIDING THAT TIME BELONGS TO YOU

Clocks slay time.

Only when the clock stops does time come to life.

—WILLIAM FAULKNER, *THE SOUND AND THE FURY*

We have given more attention to measuring time than to anything in nature. But time remains an abstraction, a riddle that exists only in our minds.

—GERNOT WINKLER, DIRECTOR OF TIME SERVICES, U.S. NAVAL OBSERVATORY

Muriel is a tall, energetic woman of striking appearance; her dark hair falls in a soft page boy, framing her animated face. She generates an air of competence about her as she talks.

Until recently, she told me, she had a job that she loved tremendously and expected to stay at forever, as manager of a photographer's studio. An entrepreneurial type with a variety of business talents, she describes herself as highly productive and desirous of doing first-rate work. Since college she had taken a variety of posts that never seemed to engage her completely. Until this job.

From the beginning, Muriel loved the job because it gave rein to all her talents. She discovered a gift for salesmanship and marketing, and her boss enthusiastically gave her the go ahead to do whatever she wanted. She worked out a tie-in with a local caterer. Every time a prospective bride and groom came to look over the reception hall, she got a referral.

Before long, the photographer had a booming business, and Muriel was as happy as a lark. She put together a sample album telling the story of an event—bar mitzvah, graduation, anniversary, and the like. Sales skyrocketed. She sold a few picture frames to the mothers of the brides, and that grew into a profitable sideline. Muriel had the Midas touch.

She began to work very long hours. A perfectionist, she went to many of the events to oversee the photographers at work.

"Yes," she admitted, "I was a bit overzealous, but I wanted to make sure everything went well, and, besides, I kept getting new ideas for more business." After working all day, Muriel would often be out at evening parties or receptions, especially on weekends. "It wasn't unusual for me to be heading home at midnight," Muriel recalled.

In her mid-thirties, she was totally immersed in the job. The lines between worklife and personal life dimmed, then disappeared. It didn't matter because she had no serious relationships. She was free, or so she told herself, to give everything to the work she loved.

One day, a grandmotherly sort came into the studio and noticed that Muriel had no ring on her finger.

"A nice young thing like you should be married," the elderly woman declared. "I know you meet plenty of men on this job, but they're already taken."

"I laughed politely," Muriel told me, "but I thought, she's right. Then I just plunged back into work and forgot about it."

Two years passed—a blur in Muriel's memory as she now thinks back on it. Then a turning point came.

It happened one summer evening when she was leaving a reception. At just past dusk, the moon was visible as it rose in the darkening sky. Walking toward her car, Muriel looked up.

"In the sky above me," said Muriel, "I saw a hawk with wings outstretched soaring through the sky. I stopped to watch him fly, his shape silhouetted against the moon. Suddenly I thought: He's free and I'm not."

That turning point changed Muriel's whole life. The next morning she went in and resigned, telling her boss that, as much as she loved it, the job allowed her no life of her own.

"He cried and I cried, but I left," Muriel said. She wanted to find a man and make a life with him. Not long afterward she took a job in journalism and met the man who became her husband.

The turning point for Muriel was the moment she decided that the time of her life belonged to her. It was up to her to become who she wanted to be.

Whose Time Do You Live?

You can't have a life of your own if you've given all your time over to others. The misery you suffer when you go from day to day carrying the heavy burden of constant time pressure can be alleviated only by going to the heart of the problem. It seems so obvious to say that our time belongs intimately to each of us—yes, of course it does. But think of this. If we spend almost every minute of every day meeting the demands made on our time by others, then our time belongs in a very real lived sense to them. How we spend our time ultimately molds us into the shape that defines us.

The first tyrant that usually robs us of our time isn't a person at all, but the clock. We are so used to equating time with the measurement of time—timekeeping instead of living time—that it's worthwhile to consider the difference. There are valid and important, indeed essential, uses for clocks. Problems arise when we unwittingly invest a clock with more power than it deserves. A clock is a mechanical device, nothing more. Time, on the contrary, is everything to us.

Are We Obsessive Timekeepers?

Obsessed with keeping time, we tend to forget that people lived time before they ever invented a machine to measure it. Now we tend to confuse the time of our lives with the timekeeping mechanisms we invented. We developed the skill to measure the passage of time by clocks to an incredible degree of accuracy, but keeping time is not the same as living our own time.

We did not invent time. But once we humans became conscious of it, we invented timekeeping. Humankind's first timepiece was the sun, traveling in a great arch across the sky from dawn to dusk, day in and day out. The need to measure time, to tell time, to keep time, is essential to human civilization, reaching back much further than our American past. The centuries-old effort to attach numbers to the passage of time parallels our evolution from simple societies to complex technologically sophisticated cultures. The Babylonians first developed a year of 360 days, then divided it into 12 lunar months of 30 days each, followed by the Egyptians, who extended the year by five days and divided the day into two 12-hour cycles.

Of course, we Americans from the beginning have been particularly vulnerable to the siren call of speed. We have also valued not only hard work and substantial productivity, but the speed with which we could build a civilization out of a wilderness.

Now the incredible accuracy of our timekeeping devices acts on us as a pressure to keep track of our own path through the day on a second-to-second, if not a nanosecond-to-nanosecond, basis. Now our timekeeping devices have far outpaced the ability of our minds to imagine their accuracy. We have atomic clocks, but we're still the same people, the same humans: children of nature's time as well as creators of a highly technological civilization.

Do Our Timekeepers Rule Us?

It is up to each of us to decide when we need to watch the clock and when we don't—how to make the clock serve our needs, rather than the reverse. What has happened is that we've let ourselves run to the clock's time rather than make the clock keep time for us, for whatever use we wish to make of it. We have created an immensely complex world of time for ourselves. In order that we not lose ourselves in this labyrinth, we need to be conscious masters of our own time, not the slaves of our timekeeping inventions.

Clocks Have Limits: They Shouldn't Run Our Lives

David Allen, a time theorist at the National Institute of Standards and Technology, points out that clocks are devices of great limitation, unrelated to the past, which "does not exist except in our memory," or the future, which does not exist "except in our expectations of it." He concludes, "The most a clock gives is the time an instant ago—not even the time now."

Allen points out, "A clock also says how long something takes. We find this intriguing, I think, because interval time—in sports, science, driving down the interstate, or in the rhythms of music, dance, and poetry— usually involves action."

In Greece during the fifth century B.C., Zeno of Elea first raised the question of how a specific interval could be divided into smaller intervals that could, in turn, be subdivided endlessly. This paradox confounds us still today, although our civilization has learned to split a second into unimaginably minuscule intervals through technology.

Modern societies have developed ever more precise measurements of time in order to serve the needs of growing technology, but the human effect of speeding us up has taken a terrible toll. It's not so much that we've made ourselves slaves to clocks, as it is that we've tried to force clocks to do for us what they can't: Give us a guide to live by.

Atomic Clocks

Austrian-born astronomer and physicist Gernot Winkler is Director of Time Services at the U.S. Naval Observatory in Washington, D.C. He is keeper of the atomic clock, the most accurate ever made by man. "Our primary job is to keep the time for the military. But our product is also for civilian use," said Winkler in a recent *National Geographic* article. "Our technological world needs the precise time. A navigator at sea or aloft, plotting his location by satellite, relies on a time signal accurate to within a single millionth of a second [microsecond]. Deep space probes like the planetary explorer Voyager II are guided by radio signals timed to billionths of a second [nanoseconds].

"And physicists tracking motion inside an atomic nucleus reckon in picoseconds [trillionths of a second] or even femtoseconds [thousandths of a picosecond]. To grasp this, consider that there are more femtoseconds in one second than there were seconds in the past 31 million years." The atomic clocks at the U.S. Naval Observatory mark the hours at the rate of 9,192,631,770 oscillations a second, like all cesium clocks.

The standard for determining the length of a second in the United States is in Boulder, Colorado. This cesium device, called the NBS-6, is the nation's most precise atomic clock. Operated by the National Institute of Standards and Technology, it is accurate to within one second in 300,000 years.

NIST scientists are now able to define a meter—the world's basic unit of distance—in terms of the time it takes light in a vacuum to travel its length: 3.33564095 nanoseconds—approximately.

Moreover, a system that traverses the globe now keeps the whole world time-synchronized. Atomic clocks at some 50 timekeeping stations from Washington and Paris to Moscow and Xian manage this remarkable feat.—John Boslaugh, "The Enigma of Time," *National Geographic*, March 1990

Don't Ask a Clock What Time Is

We shouldn't expect a clock to do what it wasn't made to do: Give our lives meaning and significance. Don't ask a clock to tell you the meaning of life. It can't. Nor can a clock tell you the meaning of time. Only you can live out the meaning of time in your life.

Time is both precious and elusive. The secret of being in tune with time, having it for a friend and ally instead of an enemy, is the prize we all seek, whether consciously or not. Like the desk clocks that are ultimately (striving to be) in synchronization with the atomic clocks, we need to have a long-range sense of our life in time.

Who are we? Where are we going? These are the basic human questions that get played out in time. The clock gives no answers. We have to look inside ourselves. Answers will begin to emerge. We will begin to get a sense of living our life in time which corresponds to the dictates of our internal rhythms, needs, and desires. Freedom is the result when we decide that the time of our life belongs to us alone.

Clock Time vs. Lived Time

The first mechanical clock is thought to have been built by an unknown ironsmith in the thirteenth century for an English monastery. The monks were called to prayer at regular intervals through the day by bells known as "cloks." The distinction then was very clear. The monks were living out their time in accordance with a clear goal: service to their God. The "cloks" were strictly a means to an end: reminding them when it was time to pray.

In our society today we've lost sight of the distinction between *clock* time and *lived* time. This is the difference you need to take hold of confidently. In reminding you that your time belongs to you, I am not referring to "clock time." I mean that your life belongs to you—each precious minute of it, and nobody else should decide how that hourglass of your life should be spent.

The next question is how to take back your time. Start with this reality: The clock is nothing more than a mechanical device, whether on the wall, on your wrist, beside your bed, or on your car dashboard. The clock doesn't own you. You own yourself. Now let us move on to the first steps that will enable you to live the fact that your time belongs to you.

Reaching the Turning Point

We can't change our lives until we decide to act. If we suffer from an extreme sense of time urgency, we feel trapped. We fear we can never get rid of the feeling. But you can throw off the burden and be free. The first step is deciding to act. You need to bring yourself to the turning point, the moment of decision.

What lies immediately before us is the present moment as it arrives. This is the moment for decision making. The past is over, although we may bring from it a rich memory harvest. The future stretches before us—a mystery of unknown days, months, years. You can't afford to wait until you have time to make changes. As playwright Eugene Ionesco pointed out, "We haven't the time to take our time." People who are time-driven have no "extra" time for themselves. And until they make changes, they probably never will. Since we all have the same time available to us, and since we have equal access to time, then it follows that there is no better time than right now to decide that time belongs to you.

You can make this decision by taking three small "mental steps." Each of these three steps below requires nothing but the assent of your mind and then the act of your will.

Three Mental Steps

1. Realize That Nobody Owns Your Time But You

We pass through life in time; our life is inseparable from our time. Nobody has the right to take that away from us. Time is our most precious possession, our most intimate companion. And yet, in succumbing to time urgency, you live as if your time belongs to others. You've given over dominion of your time to others—spouse, boss, children, errands and tasks, any stranger who wants to reach you by telephone. The list goes on. You've let slip away to others the right to command how you spend your time. Say to yourself: "My time belongs to me." As you read further in this book, you will arrive at a much deeper understanding of what this means, but for now say it again: *"My time belongs to me."*

Wayne and Sharon: Sears Doesn't Own Our Time

During the months when Sears went through the process of restructuring, Wayne's whole family lived on tenterhooks: Would his position be saved? They felt their days suspended in unreal time. Their lives were "on hold" while the corporation decided Wayne's fate. At first they were relieved that Wayne came through the first cut when hundreds of employees were fired in a single day. But he soon realized he'd only gotten a reprieve. The thinning-out of employee ranks would continue.

Wayne and Sharon sat down, once the initial panic-and-relief syndrome had passed, and talked things over. It didn't happen overnight. They had to struggle to overcome a sort of emotional paralysis that struck them. It took them weeks of conversation before they got to the decision point. With all their hearts they wanted to believe that the problem was solved and Wayne's career at Sears was safely back on course. But they served as a reality principle for each other.

Finally, they faced facts. Everything had changed. But they refused to be bulldozed. They decided their future was not in the corporation's hands. They had choices. How they spent the days of their lives was a decision that belonged to them. Together they chose to take back ownership of their time. That was Wayne and Sharon's turning point. Later they would figure out how to plan their future in new ways, independent of Sears. The essential first step was the decision to take back the reins of their life.

Kate: Aftermath of a Buyout

A 35-year-old New Yorker, Kate is a lab technologist who loved her job. When the corporate owners changed, she was grateful to be kept on when other equally competent employees were let go. She worked doubly hard, putting in overtime every week, to prove herself. Kate was shocked when management passed her over for promotion. Even worse, her boss had come to expect her to put in regular overtime. Finally, after a year of super-long hours, every one of which was miserable, she realized one day on the way to work that she had made a mistake. She had given her time over to somebody else, and she wanted it back. That moment of being jolted on the subway was Kate's turning point. She took the first mental step toward freedom.

Tony: An Early Decision Maker

Tony, the young professional in his early twenties from chapter 2, is in an ideal position. It's never too late to reach a turning point, but the earlier you do, the better off you will be. Tony got out of college just before the Wall Street crash of 1987. He got into the corporate ranks in time to hear about the bloodbaths of corporations that were involved in the merger-and-acquisition craze. He could read in the newspapers every day about all the companies jettisoning employees as the first panicky response to the threat of a takeover—or as a strategy for paying off debt incurred in a merger.

Moreover, right after he finished college, he'd had the good fortune to spend a year in Europe, where he experienced the volatility of international economics firsthand.

Tony reached a turning point very early in his corporate career. He told me that he decided to sit down and take stock of his assets. They turned out to be quite a few: Ivy League graduate with an excellent record, a year of studies abroad, terrific recommendations, and a first job with an excellent corporation. He was well placed.

But he told me, "Being well placed isn't significant in today's dynamic world. Everything is moving, and I can't afford to be static." He made the decision, at this turning point, to keep possession of his time.

"I'm keeping all my options open," is the way he put it. "I'm not putting all my eggs in the basket of this one company."

Initially he didn't work out a plan. He figured he had a little time for that. But he was correct in identifying and taking a crucial first step. The decision to retain ownership of his time and not to put his long-range career goals in the hands of his current employer was a smart move toward independence and eventual success.

"I'm going to keep my own counsel, for starters," he said, flashing a wide grin.

2. Decide to Value Your Own Time

One of the fundamental reasons you have slipped into the trap of time urgency, strangely enough—for it seems like a paradox—is that you've spent your time profligately, meeting every demand as though there were an infinite amount of time available to call upon forever. It is as though you had said: My time has no value; therefore, I will use it up without thought.

Now you need to reverse your thought to this: "My time is too precious to use up without thought." Say to yourself: "I will value my time." Your time is more precious than all the jewels in the world heaped together, because they cannot buy back a minute of your time.

Stephanie's Moment of Decision

Stephanie, burdened by all the demands on her time, was beginning to take on a slightly stoop-shouldered appearance. I noticed on one of my subsequent interviews that her eyes had the telltale darting habit. Her head and shoulders jutted forward slightly, as if she were always at-the-ready for her next task. She told me that her Sunday schedule was probably as pressured as it is any other day of the week. She cooked a lavish brunch, went to church, then did her weekly grocery shopping. While making a big dinner, she ran upstairs and downstairs to do the laundry. In the evenings, she worked on long-range planning for her job as magazine features editor.

One Sunday afternoon, however, when Steve was gone for the day, Stephanie suddenly decided to abandon her schedule and took the baby to the city fair. They ate hot dogs, rode the merry-go-round, drove the kiddie cars, and in the midst of having a wonderful time, Stephanie got struck as if by a lightning bolt. The contrast between the bonding she and Michelle experienced that day, and the usual Sunday drudgery, was so dramatic that she decided, like the Biblical pearl of great price, to treat her time with the value it truly had. On that Sunday afternoon at the fair, she resolved to get off the time treadmill. She knew it would take time to figure out how to do it. But the resolution was made. This was her turning point.

Jason: He Deserved a Career Too

When he first learned that his elderly and disabled parents would be moving to the city where he had a demanding job as a newspaper editor, Jason could hardly keep up with all the practical details of making the arrangements. Once this first stage was over, however, he sank into depression.

It seemed to him that his future was nothing but an endless stream of days during which he was constantly at the beck and call of his parents, while struggling to get through a huge and hopeless pile of papers, unedited feature articles, and telephone messages that were out of control on his desk. He lost, for a while, all sense of having any life of his own, much less any time of his own.

The turning point came for Jason when his old college roommate, the best friend he'd ever had, dropped into town unexpectedly and swung over to the newspaper office.

He was shocked by the change in his friend, Jason. He couldn't believe how dispirited his friend had become, when he had been a dynamo of energy before. He dragged out of Jason that he was in a terrible state of conflict, believing that the only relief he would ever have was when both parents were dead. Then he was horrified to think of himself wishing his parents dead.

Jason's friend convinced him that it was possible to find alternatives to the problem. It wasn't necessary to totally turn over his own time to his disabled parents. With his friend's help, Jason reached the turning point of deciding that his time belonged to him, and he was going to figure out how to get it back—without abandoning his parents.

3. Recognize That You Have Choices

It isn't enough simply to realize that time belongs to you, that time is precious and needs to be valued by you. The final step in your mental liberation is to actively face the fact that you do have choices. I've found almost invariably in my conversations with time-driven people that, however much they yearn to be in charge of their own time, *they believe earnestly that they can't change a single item in their schedules.* They put up tremendous roadblocks to their own freedom. They make up a list of reasons a mile long as to why they don't have choices and why they must stay on the time treadmill.

This is a slave mentality, an addict's reaction. We victimize ourselves by wrapping mental chains around ourselves. It is not other people who must release us. We must grant ourselves freedom. We must give ourselves permission to be free. A friend of mine, a gifted poet, once told me that this was how she released the torrent of words from her subconscious: "I gave myself permission to write poetry," she said, and in some inexplicable way, it worked.

Overcoming Blind Spots

Sometimes the more miserable we are, the more resistant to change we become; it is one of those strange quirks of human nature that defy rational explanation. Here are the most common excuses I've heard from people who resist confronting their turning point:

- "I don't have time to think about anything."
- "If I don't do it, nobody will."
- "There's no other way to do it."
- "My boss insists that I do this."
- "Everybody expects me to do all I do."
- "I couldn't get another job if I tried."
- "My husband won't change."
- "I've tried before, and nothing works."
- "There's no alternative."
- "It's too late."
- "I'll lose my job."
- "My wife won't change."
- "Things will soon get better."

This resistance to change, especially when it arises in a time-pressured situation, is understandable. You can overcome these blind spots by yourself, with a will, but it can be helpful if someone near and dear can help. Give that person a chance.

Lucky Couples

Paul and Barbara and Larry and Diane are among the couples who are lucky to have one person in the marriage who is a time-integrated person who is able to help the other one see the distortion that has invaded their lives. In many cases, when both husband and wife experience severe time urgency, it's the blind leading the blind as far as finding a solution goes. Not all couples are willing to face up to these problems. But in these two families, the wives persisted in trying to convince their husbands that they did have a choice.

Said Diane, "I made Larry sit down and watch the TV program which told about the Japanese women who were widowed in their 30s when their husbands died of overworking—simply spending too many hours on the job."

But Larry added, "I made the decision to take back control of my time. Unless I'd made that decision for myself, everything Diane said would have fallen on deaf ears. I guess I just woke up one morning and said to myself, 'This has got to change. It's a rat race and I'm sick of it.'"

Diane retorted, "Well, I don't care who made him see; the big thing is that he now realizes it's up to him to do something. I think he will."

With Paul and Barbara, the situation was different. Paul had been more entrenched in his heavy weekday/getaway weekend pattern than Larry. Besides, he had been doing it for more years, and for a number of them, had persisted in a pattern of denial. Until you see for yourself that you have choices, and want to change, nobody can do it for you. But Barbara persisted. She tried to choose times, during their getaways, when Paul was relaxed and rested, to raise the question.

"It took over a year," Barbara told me. "I wasn't going to give up, because it's our life, our whole future at stake. I didn't want to live with a man who perpetually fell asleep in the middle of a sentence on the sofa. Besides, I felt he would finally kill himself if he didn't change."

Paul can't really account for his choice.

"It mattered to me that Barbara was getting very unhappy," Paul said. "If she said there was a problem, I figured there must be one."

Barbara recalled, "I kept asking him, 'Who is making you do this?' and he couldn't answer. I guess I just wore him down to the point where he realized that his time on the job had turned into a big problem between us."

"That's it," said Paul. "For myself I would have gone on this way till I dropped. I never felt I deserved consideration. But for Barbara, well I love her and I could see she was miserable, so I decided to make changes."

Paul's feeling that he didn't, on his own merits, deserve consideration, I recognized as a common attitude among people who suffer from extreme time urgency. This belief stems from a lack of self-esteem, which helps precipitate one into the time trap, then helps keep one there. He was fortunate that Barbara helped him see the light.

Three Steps Can Change Everything

Taken together, these three steps constitute the turning point when a person decides to take back the time that rightfully belongs to him or her. What is important at this starting point is not *how* you will do it; the methods for solving the time problem come later. First, decide you will do it. Almost everybody who suffers from extreme time urgency occasionally gets a break, however brief, which shows him or her how precious time is and how much different freedom is from slavery. But what most often happens is that a person like Stephanie might say, "How wonderful the day was—I'll have to do that again sometime." Nothing changes.

To take back your time is to experience your time from within yourself, not to regard your life from the outside as a continuum of quantifiable units. Your time belongs to you so that you can be who you are, who you want to be. To own yourself is to allow yourself to return to your inner sense of your unique reality. The turning point is to decide to enter into a deeper realization of your life's meaning. It's to say to yourself: That's who I am—my time.

The Way In Is the Way Out

The philosopher Ludwig Wittgenstein suggested that whenever we find ourselves trapped, as if in a room where no windows or other means of exit are apparent, we need only turn around and notice that the door which brought us into this place still stands open. The way in is also the way out.

To recover from Urgency Addiction, those who suffer from it need to get off the time treadmill, to follow a path which leads to a renewed sense of self, a freedom to enjoy one's success. The object of the effort to reclaim one's time is to get back one's very self, lost in the constant minute-by-minute struggle against the clock.

Time Gains

In reading this far, you have already taken several important steps toward freedom:

- You have diagnosed the areas in your life in which Urgency Addiction is weighing you down.
- You have recognized the various cultural and personal forces which have caused you to fall into the time trap.
- You have decided that time belongs to you.

Now you will get a road map to help you get back to the main path. This map will enable you to keep and even enhance the success you have already earned, but at the same time, allow you to throw away the excessive time worries which have put a damper on your enjoyment of life. You will regain the freedom to succeed not only in your career, but in your personal life as well. You will regain the time of your life.

7

TRAITS OF SUCCESSFUL, TIME-INTEGRATED PEOPLE

Time present and time past

Are both perhaps present in time future,

And time future contained in time past.

—T.S. ELIOT, "BURNT NORTON"

What is it that characterizes people who are free of time urgency? They seem to know the secret of living time well. I wondered why it was that, of two people who were equally busy, one of them seemed obviously harried and time-driven, whereas the other appeared self-possessed, at ease with himself. I set out to discover what traits these time-integrated people, as I call them, possessed which distinguished them from their time-pressured counterparts.

I wasn't interested in people who were merely busy and merely successful, but rather (rarer birds!) in busy, successful people who lived out their time in harmony with themselves. I sought out people who were running their own race, rather than careening out of control down a runway that stripped them of all deep enjoyments. I looked for successful people who radiated happiness in both their personal and career lives. I wanted to find out their secrets. In my search, I used only one criterion: the person had to be very busy. If a person had no sense of time urgency because he or she wasn't busy, then I had nothing to learn from that individual.

Eventually, I recognized seven traits that distinguish time-integrated people. It became clear that their attitudes toward time expressed fundamental attitudes toward themselves, and were, in fact, indistinguishable from the way they lived their lives. Their profound acceptance of time— observable in their behavior—arose from an unshakable sense of self-worth. Although they had a variety of careers and personalities, they shared a common set of values and patterns of behavior.

Seven Traits of Time-Integrated People

People who are time-integrated relate to the wholeness of time, inter-weaving carefully and constructively the fluid threads of past, present, and future. They live out of a sense of purpose grounded in time; they have an unerring sense of who they are in the flow of time. This sense of being grounded in time gives them self-confidence, a resistance to whims and worries of the moment, a steady perspective on life. I saw their wholeness as a kind of seamless garment that they wear through their days. But I tried to identify the elements which were so carefully woven into this flowing garment of time. Eventually, I recognized seven traits of time-integrated people which manifest themselves in character-istic behavior observable to an onlooker:

1. They Never Seem to Be in a Hurry

They aren't clock monitors. They don't continually glance at their watches. They listen to themselves. Time-integrated people run their own race. They don't allow themselves to sink into a state of constant time urgency. They set their own pace, regardless of others' expectations, and somehow convince the world around them to accept them on their own terms. Simultaneously, they seem aware of being in the flow of time, feeling the present slide smoothly into the future while the past eases into the background. They allow events in their lives to unfold at a natural pace, marking along the way the interconnecting skeins of past and fu-ture. They seem balanced, living according to their own inner rhythms. Even their body language tends to be graceful and purposeful, not jerky and rushed. No matter how important and elevated their status, they don't make you feel that you're intruding on their time.

2. They Experience the Present Moment to the Fullest

Time-integrated people exhibit outstanding powers of concentration and an uncanny capacity to focus on the moment they inhabit and the tasks as well as the fulfillment it brings. This quality appears both in work and play. When absorbed in a work project, they give themselves over totally to it. So, too, in their leisure and recreation time. They demonstrate a joyful and exuberant gift for laughter, pleasure, enjoyment to the hilt. They can let go and have fun spontaneously. But this is not the same as losing oneself in the vapid diversions of the moment. They are not es-capists, always hurrying things along out of a voracious appetite to con-sume experiences at an ever accelerating rate. Their concern is not with the quantity of experiences, but the quality of them. They can squeeze the maximum amount of intensity, awareness, absorption, knowledge, and emotional fulfillment out of the moment as they live it. They know how to make a minute last forever. Looking you directly in the face, they make you feel that you have their full attention, and that nothing matters more to them than listening to what you say.

3. They Believe They Deserve Time for Themselves

Egoism is not a mark of the time-integrated person. The sense of self-worth which inspires one to take personal time is quite the opposite of selfishness. It stems from an awareness of one's dignity and essential worth as a unique human being. Time-integrated people know who they are. Accordingly, they take time to nurture themselves. They believe in their responsibility to preserve their health, their mental and emotional well-being, and—most of all—their creative resources. They avoid operating at the edge of their capacities, but seek ways to continually replenish their inner vitality. They don't permit others, willy-nilly, to define how they spend their days, for they understand that what they do with their time is inseparable from who they are as persons.

4. They Make Time to Get What They Want

People who are time-integrated have a sense of purpose. They refuse to let any impediment stand in the way of their goals. They believe that they have the right to arrange their time to fit in the things they want to do. Not only do they set strong goals, they also exhibit the flexibility to work around obstacles, negotiate difficult terrain, handle the unexpected. They don't permit setbacks to demolish them emotionally. They don't let disappointments distract them from their objectives. Whenever they are unavoidably thrown offtrack, they keep this interrupted time at a minimum and return to using their own time for their own purposes as soon as they reasonably can. Because they experience the present in which they live as purposeful, they are not easily thwarted by unexpected events in life. They can bring to bear all their resources to handle the difficulties that spring up. As a result, they seem to accomplish more than other people with the same amount of time at their disposal.

5. They Welcome the Future with Confidence

People who are time-integrated don't fear the future, nor do they live in constant anticipation of deadlines, due dates, obligations, and responsibilities, whether tomorrow, next year, or five years ahead. They realize that life is process, that change supplies the opportunity for growth, that whatever the future brings, they will be open and flexible. They don't hurry the future toward them. Their chief focus is on the present as it rolls along toward the future—whatever still lies ahead for constructive and fulfilling action. This very American trait, perhaps the source of our special creative genius, is to look at the future with hope. We can choose to live out our time with regard to the future either as passive victims, waiting for events to happen, or oblivious to what lies ahead, like an unthinking child, or with conscious resolve and determination. We can choose to become our best selves, our truest selves in the future, whatever events may bring us. Time-integrated people are not at the mercy of the future: they actively embrace it as an ally.

6. They Create a Rich, Usable Past

Memories are a source of strength and guidance for time-integrated people. They don't waste the precious flow of time in their lives by negative thoughts about the past—guilt, anger, regret, self-blame, or blame of others. Nor do they disown the past, attempting to bury it as if it never existed. They take steps to resolve the conflicts which could make them prisoners of past actions and events. Knowing that the past is irretrievable, they wisely lay their private ghosts to rest and move on. They regard the past in a positive way—as a rich harvest of experience, lessons, even an unfolding source of secrets that may enhance the present. The past is a container which holds many things—bad, good, and indifferent. It is up to us to construct out of that past a usable entity that makes our present going into the future more substantial and meaningful, not weighted down by baggage. Time-integrated people don't cast off the past, failing to heed its call of conscience, if such be the case. They don't carelessly turn their backs on the past as if it were a used-up present to be tossed on a garbage pile. The past always has potentially more to offer, and time-integrated people often use that resource in their search for life's answers.

7. They Spend Time on Relationships That Matter

As much as they may enjoy all the good things in life, people who are time-integrated seek to increase the time spent with worthwhile people—both in their personal lives, with family and friends, and in their career lives. Just as they recognize the importance of nurturing themselves, they also know how to cultivate their circle of caring people. They assertively seek out mentors for their career development and keep connected to business associates far beyond the confines of their own workplaces. They renew relationships with old friends and distant family members. They respond warmly to new acquaintances who offer them a chance to grow and expand their horizons. They don't crassly use other people. They don't cynically regard others as instruments to further their own success. Nor do they allow themselves to be used by others. They are willing both to teach and to learn, as well as to care and to be cared for. Time-integrated people realize that when people matter, they need to express their feelings primarily by spending time with them.

How Can I Get These Traits?

That was what I asked myself when I realized how desirable it is to be a time-integrated person. It seemed that these people, above all, were free. They had an ease and zest about them that appealed tremendously to me. They lived the way I wanted to live. I became convinced along the way that all the traits of a time-integrated person can be acquired. Every person I interviewed told me that the traits were conscious and willed. It obviously required effort to become time-integrated, of course, but it was worthwhile. Above all, I wanted to get rid of the awful burden of time urgency. We have the freedom, if only we recognize it, to make choices about time. Let me describe a few of the many people who taught me what time integration means. Among them are some I did not personally meet; most of them, however, talked with me at length.

Oprah and Dolly: Time Is on Their Side

While I was working on this book and thinking about the qualities of a time-integrated person, I flipped on the TV one afternoon and tuned in to *The Oprah Show*. I love to watch Oprah Winfrey because I remember her from earlier days in Baltimore before she became a star. I wrote a feature article on her while she was co-host of a local morning talk show. At the studio where I interviewed her, she was very low key and reticent; the interview included her co-host, Richard Sher, who like to have the upper hand with her, and also the station publicist, whose presence tended to dampen the spontaneity of our conversation.

But I was struck by Oprah's rich, vibrant voice, and even more by her unhurried sense of purpose. She told me that she intended to be an actress someday, and that she believed everything happens at the time it should: life is process. Seeing her talent, even though it was somewhat buried under a bushel then, I figured she was biding her time. Not long after that, she got the offer to host her own show in Chicago. She was *ready for it*. She seized the moment and let her personality blossom. Now, of course, she has also made significant strides as an actress. I can't help thinking she is still biding her time—the process keeps unfolding naturally.

As I watched her recently on TV, Oprah was chatting with the stars of the movie *Steel Magnolias:* Shirley MacLaine, Darryl Hannah, Olympia Dukakis, Julia Roberts, and Dolly Parton. I was mesmerized by Dolly, whose immediacy before the cameras makes her a riveting presence. In the middle of the conversation, Dolly suddenly announced to the other stars (and to millions of us viewers): "I'm a very spiritual person." She spoke with such candid simplicity that I believed her instantly. Shirley MacLaine was sitting nearby, and for once, her mouth dropped open mutely. Shirley had written books about going to distant mountaintops in search of spirituality, but it seemed that Dolly had it right inside her and all she had to do was open herself up and let it out.

The next day I bought a couple of her tapes and played them. What attracted me were the songs she, herself, had composed. I felt that I knew her intimately from the first song. It hit me that at the very heart of her artistry was her understanding of the flow of time in her life. Out of her past she has created wonderful music.

Dolly Parton grew up poor in the Smoky Mountains of Tennessee. With her parents and 10 brothers and sisters, she lived in a tiny, two-bedroom country cabin set on 75 acres. For several years she and her siblings shared one bedroom, sleeping two or three to a bed. Around the fireplace the family used to listen to the Grand Ole Opry on the radio long before she dreamed of singing there herself. What's outstanding about Dolly Parton is not that she triumphed and became a star in spite of her poor childhood, but that she reached into that past for inspiration that has flowered richly in her songs. She got down deep into her child-hood roots, explored the many-colored feelings she discovered there, and out of those memories created the lilting harmony of her music.

Calling up the hills of Tennessee in summertime, she wrote the hit song, "My Tennessee Mountain Home," in which images of life "as peace-ful as a baby's sigh," were interwoven with images of honeysuckle, song-bird, and soaring eagle. "The Coat of Many Colors" became a tribute to her mother, who made her a coat she loved out of colorful scraps of fabric from the ragbag; in this song she draws on her religious past (her grand-father was a preacher) with an implicit reference to the Biblical story of Joseph and his many-colored coat. One of Dolly's most-loved metaphors is the butterfly which holds many secrets. In "Love Is Like a Butterfly," she blends her love of nature and people with her memories of childhood to create an intensely lyrical song. Once, as a small child, she noticed the little many-colored butterfly flitting across the meadow, and from that single image eventually wrote a beautiful song. This is how an artist creates a usable past.

For Dolly Parton, the past of childhood memories is a deep well from which she draws inspiration and nourishment for her musical talents. Far from trying to disown or abandon her past, she repeatedly discovers new riches there. I've found that a person can have this grounding in the past naturally—by character or family background, or perhaps temperament, or a combination of these things. Although few people can command Dolly's musical gifts, anybody can draw inspiration from his or her past. Often I've observed, as with Dolly Parton, that the quality of time integration is spiritually based in people, identified with their deepest beliefs about the meaning of life.

Outside Ordinary Time: A Shattering Conversation

Sometimes a person can get lucky early in life and discover a deeper meaning of time—and friendship.

Phil Riggio was an 18-year-old college student in Maryland when, after his freshman year, he took a trip alone to New Zealand for the three months of summer. He had thought one of his friends would go, too, but they all had to work.

"I really wanted to travel somewhere far away," Phil told me. "I went into a ski shop one day and heard a guy talking with this accent and I got to talking to him. He was the friendliest guy I ever met." It turned out he was a New Zealander, and he sold Phil on his country; he said it was small, the exchange rate was really good, there was skiing in mountains and surfing at beautiful beaches. Moreover, it was safe to hitchhike, and really friendly. That was important to an 18-year-old going on his own.

Phil saved up money by working in a gas station. As soon as he had enough for a ticket, he went out and bought it. Then he put out a flyer seeking a ride to Los Angeles.

"A guy from my own college answered the ad and I hoped it would be an enjoyable ride," Phil said, "but the other guy just wanted to get there, and so we drove hard for three and a half days. He was absorbed in his summer internship plans. He had a whole schedule he had to kick off for the summer. The ride he gave me was just to split expenses. We arrived there with no more bond of friendship than when we left."

This was ironic in light of the friendships he would find on the other side of the world. On the plane ride to New Zealand it began with people who took him under their wings. When they landed in Auckland, the "City of Sails," where thousands of sailboats are moored in the harbor,

Phil's new friends took him out to lunch and helped him find a youth hostel; he immediately fell in love with the beautiful city.

He began island hopping within a few days and was continually amazed at the friendly spirit of New Zealanders. When hitchhiking, he discovered, "After two or three cars go by, you have a ride. That broke the ice, and I thought, 'Geez, this is easy.'"

Phil kept a steady traveling pace. Back in Auckland, he took the bus outside the city and headed north to the citrus-growing areas. "I stayed in hostels and in a lot of people's houses," Phil said. "I was treated like family, given dinner; they even did my dirty laundry."

Later, heading south, he took his surfboard, which he carried in its own backpack. When he got to the beach, however, it was a kind of rainy day; the beach was deserted and the campground closed.

"I walked along the beach. I went up to some people and asked them if they knew anyplace to stay. I banged on a couple of doors. I'd introduce myself, say I was willing to do chores, was trustworthy, and ask if I could have a piece of toast. This one couple—Ron and his girlfriend—took me in. We talked for a while, and then Ron said, 'Here's a few dollars. Run to the store, pick us up a newspaper and milk, and we'll think over about your staying here.'"

It turned out that the New Zealander couple's only hesitation was that they were going away overnight and didn't know about leaving Phil alone in their house. But when he got back from the store, they told him he could stay.

"It was a really nice beachfront house, with everything you could want—stereo and records. They said I should help myself. While they were gone, I cleaned the whole house, really made it spotless."

This was the kind of reception he found everywhere. I asked Phil if he had been such an outgoing type back in the States. "No," he replied, "I wasn't at all that type. I was nervous at first, but I saw it was all up to me. It would be as good or as bad as I made it. One of the gutsiest things I did was to go up and bang on doors. I made myself more outgoing. If I were to come home and find the doors of my own house locked and my parents away, I wouldn't think to ask the neighbors if I could stay overnight."

Phil went on, "The fact that *nobody* could come along with me on the trip was a blessing in disguise. I met a ton of people. Also, I was free. I decided I'd just wake up and go wherever my heart desired. But I was never alone. There were always people at youth hostels ready to talk. I kept running into the same people all over the place: the backpackers." These travelers, mostly young, were men and women from many countries—Germany, Ireland, England, Switzerland, Scotland.

One of the backpackers whom Phil encountered several times turned out to be special. James was from a farm in Iowa, about 22 years old, had graduated from college, saved money, and was now traveling around the world.

"I had seen him in North Island at a backpackers' lodge," Phil recalled. "When I first met him, I thought he was kind of dorky, insecure, and looking for attention. I didn't really like him."

Two months later, at Te-anau in fjord country, "I met him again. We really didn't have much to say. We exchanged small talk. Basically we wrote each other off. I assumed I would never see him again."

But not long afterward, again in fjord country, Phil undertook one of his most challenging hikes—a 6,000-foot climb up the majestic Mount Luxmore, which took about eight hours. "George, who was the hostel keeper, came along to watch out for me because I was feeling kind of sick that morning. There was a beautiful view of mountains and lakes as we made the ascent through the trees. George came along to the top, then left when I got there."

Phil found himself entirely alone in the traveler's hut at the top of Mount Luxmore. In the evening, a darkness and quiet descended all around him such as he had never experienced before. "Now all is dark," he wrote in his journal. "There is amazing solitude, peace and quiet."

Phil asked himself: Am I feeling lonesome?

"No, not at all," came the answer.

Outside it was pitch black. It seemed to Phil as if he were all alone in the vast natural universe of forest, trees, and mountain. He had never heard such silence.

Suddenly, James walked in. "There he was in the hut with me. Until now I had considered him a total moron," Phil recalled.

But everything changed. "James and I had a simply shattering conversation. We sat across from each other at the table in candlelight, and we were 100-percent honest with each other. Outside a wind came up and it got rainy and chilly. We had a coal-burning stove and cooked oatmeal and stuff." It was an atmosphere in which these two young men were together, surrounded by nature but no other human beings. All barriers fell away.

"That night we talked two or three hours," said Phil. "We were outside an ordinary time frame. We had no obligations whatsoever. Both of us could have sat there for days on end. It was kind of timeless. Before we knew it, hours had passed.

"We struck a chord there. We were sitting in this hut in the mountains alone. We didn't have to worry about others judging the honesty of our conversation. We had absolutely nothing to worry about— neither of us had to go anywhere the next morning—we had no itinerary that we had to follow. We straightforwardly told each other what we were thinking."

In this extraordinary exchange, Phil reversed his opinion of James. "He was struggling with himself. He was just basically searching. He sparked me into thinking how real and genuine he was. He showed me his writing. He writes extremely well. And I'd been thinking of him as a backwards farmer kid. Almost a moron."

James had been wrong about Phil, too. "He thought I was a typical rich American kid funded by his parents, just doing the trip so I could say what I'd seen. I had left a previous hostel without paying him back the six dollars I owed him. The reason I hadn't was that he wasn't awake when I left and I didn't feel like waiting around. But that reinforced his feeling that I was careless."

That evening, outside an ordinary time frame, a friendship was forged. Phil described it: "I felt different after our experience. I felt like gold. And now I can really relate to him. He is so whole. He said to me, 'You really have a good head on your shoulders.' That made me feel so damn good. For the first time I didn't feel I had to prove myself with words. I'd always felt I needed to prove that I wasn't a blockhead."

Two years later, the friendship endures. "A bond was formed between us," Phil said. "He writes to me and says, 'Take care of yourself, brother.'"

Phil wishes he could hold on to that deeper sense of time which gave rise to such a genuine friendship. "The European time frame—I fell in love with it in New Zealand," he remarked. "I had a block of three months to do whatever I wanted. It reminds me of the time back in childhood, in the old neighborhood, during the summers. There were days on end to be with people, a timeless feeling. We went skateboarding, there was a real bond among us.

"There was no big checklist: I have to see to this and this and this. In New Zealand I ended up staying at a farm for a few days with a family who invited me to dinner. I never expected to be half a world away and be treated like family. I came back really different."

Although he's tried to keep a deeper sense of time, he admitted wistfully, "I've kind of regressed. I bought right back into American time. I had anxiety that I wasn't developing friendships. I became incredibly grade-conscious. Here there's always something in the back of your mind that has to be done. I never go more than a few hours when I'm not thinking about the next thing I have to do."

Phil paused. "Everybody has their schedule. They block out their feelings. They think of the next deadline instead of their lives." When Phil said this, I thought: Here's a perfect description of time urgency.

Now Phil is looking forward to his junior year in Leuven, Belgium. He likes the setup compared to American colleges. "It's not as regimented. There are no tests, no quizzes. You're not registered until you take the final exam. At Leuven, time is different. One day kind of blends into the next.

All the students who were there last year came back with a bond." That's what Phil wants, too.

"I Don't Like to Feel Rushed"

It's not only idealistic students who yearn for a way of living their time which expresses deep meaning. Paul Rivas is a brilliant, 35-year-old internist who feels the same way. He knew what he wanted out of life when he was Phil Riggio's age in college. He took steps to plan his time so that he could accomplish his goals.

Paul and his wife, Natalie, were sweethearts in college. When they decided to get married, they agreed that the central focus of their life together would be each other and the children they hoped to raise.

Early in his medical school training, Paul declared that he would arrange his practice so that he could have plenty of time with his family. He told his plans to the psychiatrist who was tracking his whole class. Every time he talked about these values, the psychiatrist would say, " I really worry about you."

But he wasn't swayed, although he realized he was going against the grain. The average physician may spend 60 to 70 hours a week on his practice. Now he's been in practice for six years and is the father of three young children.

"I work about 30 hours a week," Paul told me, "probably the fewest hours of any internist I know."

But that's the way he wants it. "I didn't want my kids growing up not knowing me. I had a fear of my kids growing up and then my having to ask where all the time went."

He feels satisfied that he is living according to his own values. "Primarily I wanted to spend a lot of time with my family," said Paul. "So I asked myself: How do I do this? I set up my financial goals and then decided to live within that. Our income is perfectly good. Many doctors have a tendency to overbuy, to overextend themselves financially."

He limited his income deliberately in order to buy time for himself. Yet he still enjoys an excellent quality of living. He and Natalie built a home in a lovely country/suburban setting near his medical office. Natalie is free to stay home with the children, as they both wanted, and they have a rich family life together.

How does Paul arrange his practice? He relies on his receptionist, Barbara, who manages the time slots for patients in a very flexible way. They have 15-minute time periods in the appointment book, but, says Paul, "Barbara gets to know our patients and how long they require. For example, the elderly need to get a good block of time, maybe a half hour, since they usually have multiple problems, but we don't worry about it. On the other hand, a 20-year-old with a cold won't need more than 5 or 10 minutes.

"We get a feel for the problem; we have no specific block," he says. "We try to get a feel for the person."

In fact, Paul has very carefully thought through the way he spends time with patients, based on a philosophy of respect for the patients' time and needs as well as his own. "I don't like to make people wait," he remarks, "so we have 15-minute blocks, but keep them sort of loose."

He's in the office from 9 A.M. to 1 P.M. Monday, Wednesday, and Friday, as well as Thursday evening, for as long as it takes, seeing only about 10 or 12 patients during each session. He's the medical director of a nursing home with 150 patients, so he usually makes his rounds at the hospital or nursing home after his office hours. He's home by 3 or 4 P.M. most weekdays.

Paul remarked to me, "You have to start out the way I did consciously, or else you get too busy. I just set a limit and refuse to go above it."

He realizes most physicians put in more than double his number of weekly hours. "It's a greed factor," he told me. "You don't *have* to work 60 hours."

I asked Paul if other physicians think his way of practicing medicine is strange. He laughed.

"Yes, but I think there's a lot of envy. I sense a fair amount of envy. Most doctors don't spend a lot of time with their families."

He continued, "Doctors tend to define themselves in terms of medicine—as if their technical knowledge as physicians encompassed the entire definition of who they are. The ego gets pumped all through school, they get all A's, then they join a lot of committees and feel they're very successful. Once they become doctors, they need to keep on getting A's on their report card. Now the A's are their patients and money."

Paul says he doesn't have those ego needs. "I like to be relaxed in both areas—personal and professional. I don't like stress anywhere. I don't like to feel rushed, and I don't rush the patients."

Paul was raised in a family-centered way and appreciated that. "My mom stayed at home and was always with me. My father, who was an attorney, rarely stayed at his office past 5 P.M. He spent tons of time with me. Every single evening he and I would do things together, play tennis, whatever." He's sure that the time his parents spent with him influenced him favorably in his own choices.

Paul told me there are two equally important factors which enable him to lead a time-integrated life with his family: "being willing to limit my income, plus avoiding the politics of medicine."

He explains, "I get involved in none of the politics of medicine, every-thing to do with the insurance and so on. These professional societies, like the AMA and the Society for Internal Medicine, have for their main purpose to keep physicians well-reimbursed. They want to make sure that fees remain high and reimbursement schedules stay high. This is especially true of Medicare, where there are always proposals to try to limit fees."

Paul has observed that many physicians fall unthinkingly into a 60-hour or 70-hour week because they think that equals dedication. "You can still do a pretty good job as a doctor doing 70 hours a week if that's basically all you do," he said. "Most physicians just do that and nothing else." He added with a chuckle, "They're almost doctors from birth."

When the Present Moment Is Forever

Sister Angela Mary is an American nun of the Holy Cross order who has spent 25 years in Saõ Paulo, Brazil, working with the poorest of the poor in the infamous slums called *favelas*. What strikes people who observe her in action is the way she gives total concentration to the task and person at hand. I asked her on one of her home visits to America recently if that was the way she related to the Brazilian children in the *favelas*. She said yes. It was a decision she made based on her belief in the absolute worth of every human being: "I may not pass this way again. Let me give everything to this person *now.*"

But Sister Angela didn't think her ministry was difficult compared to that of some of her fellow missionaries.

She told me the story of Nanuka, the nickname of a Paraguayan nun who belonged to the Oblates of St. Benedict. She dedicated her life to working with the street people of Saõ Paulo. These missionary sisters switched from their original ministry of sheltering the homeless to going right into the streets. The shelter ministry proved overwhelming because of the numbers—some 600,000 children alone live in the streets of Saõ Paulo. Their goal became simply to help the people attain a sense of self-worth right where they were.

When she was around 40, Nanuka contracted cancer and died. A week afterwards, a memorial service was held in a church that had been con-verted from an old theater, and all the street people from the neighbor-hood—perhaps 500 men, women, and children—crowded in there, along with a few priests and nuns. Everybody sat on the floor and sang through the Mass. Then the priest, a young, bearded missionary, invited people to speak out in testimony of Nanuka. As people stepped forward hesitantly and began to speak of their beloved Nanuka, sobbing broke out among the congregation.

Finally, the last person hobbled up to the altar. He was an alcoholic in rags, a young man withered into a premature old age. His shirt was tied together, his bare feet were thickly callused. He turned to the people and held up his sandals before them.

"I offer these sandals up for what Nanuka taught me," he said in a quavery voice. "She taught me to walk. She would say, 'Zé, would you pay the light bill or the water bill for me?' and I'd say, 'Sure, Nanuka, just give me the carfare.' And she'd say, 'No Zé, you walk, but walk with God. Look at the people nearby who are rushing around, and you sit down against a building and rest, and pray that these people reach their destination. While you are praying, meditate on the legs God gave you so you can walk.'"

Zé shifted his feet, and stopped, stricken with grief for the one person who had spoken to his humanity. Then he continued, "Nanuka would say to me, 'And then get up and walk a little longer. And while you are walking, look up at the sky. Breathe the air. And remember how God loves you.' That's how Nanuka taught me to walk," said Zé, and he left his sandals at the altar.

Three Decisions about Time

Time is what we make of it. As a start in becoming a time-integrated person, make three decisions about what your attitude toward time will be from now on. Here are three statements which I like, but you may prefer others: 1. I will not be time's plaything. 2. I will listen to what's happening in the moment I'm inhabiting. 3. I will not be swayed by the urgent time demands of others. To arrive at a condition of wholeness requires small but significant steps.

8

THERE'S TIME ENOUGH (FOR EVERYTHING THAT MATTERS)

Thus we play the fools with time;

and the spirits of the wise

sit in the clouds and mock us.

—SHAKESPEARE, *HENRY IV*

Nobody gets everything in life. But most of us can have everything that matters. People who suffer from time urgency are usually getting very little or nothing of what really matters. Often we are too busy to notice what is missing. Most people who suffer from excessive time urgency have accumulated responsibilities over a period of time. We got buried beneath a heap of demands made on our time by others. In struggling to meet every expectation, we divided time up into smaller and smaller segments so as to squeeze out every bit of productivity. We end up feeling more harried than ever. We're not getting at the heart of the matter.

Deciding What Matters

In order to get what we want in life, we must first decide what truly matters to us. This means sitting down in a quiet place alone and assessing basic values, goals, desires, and relationships. If you are suffering from time urgency, you have been so busy accomplishing the tasks on your list, running faster and faster to get more and more things done, that you probably can't remember the last time you really thought about yourself.

Who are you? Who do you want to be? Who are you on your way to becoming? These are the questions that will lead to satisfying answers. When I made this suggestion to one of the time-driven executives I was interviewing, he gave me a startled look. "That's very scary," he said. "I

haven't looked into myself in years. I don't know what I'd find there."
Exactly.

Making a Clearing

Think of the old wilderness days of America when pioneers trudged
deep into the virgin forests, staked out a piece of land to settle on, and
made a clearing. This clearing was a physical space within which they
built not only a home but a new life for themselves: a profound spiritual
purpose animated the rough-hewn cabins and sheds. This is the double
sense in which you want to make a clearing for yourself. You want to
start with a literal clearing of your calendar to give you a free 15 or 30
minutes of undisturbed time. But that is just the start. You need to carve
out a broad mental space that allows you to breathe fresh air. After
all, this is a new beginning, a new time for you. I emphasize the need to
have a mental clearing because this is exactly what you lack as a time-
pressured person. You have a desperate need to focus, to concentrate, to
be at home with yourself. How else will you ever find out who you are
and what really matters to you?

Give complete attention to yourself within this time you set aside.
You are making a clearing for yourself, a mental space that is all yours.
It will be *from within* this clearing that you will decide what matters. You
will come face to face with yourself. We will then build on the experiences you will have in this space. You will be able to take away from this
space important new perceptions of yourself and your time.

Stake Out a Special Place

Like the pioneers, build a little cabin all for yourself. Have a place—a
small room, a corner of a room, a favorite chair—it doesn't matter how
big or how small. What matters is that it is the purely personal space you
will inhabit to pay attention exclusively and completely to yourself.
You will come back to this place, this figurative rustic cabin, again and
again. You will find quite soon that this space acquires a meaning. The
good feelings associated with your giving desperately needed time to
yourself will spring up spontaneously. The last thing you probably ever
have as a time-driven person is a time and a place just for your personal
self. You have used up every inch of mental space as you made your time
maximally productive. In the process, you have misplaced your own self
and need to find that self again.

Here is your strategy. Go to this chosen place, equipped with pad and
pencil. Make sure nobody will disturb you. Sit down and relax. Don't fret

if the whole process seems awkward; that's natural at first. Now clear your head of all your worries, plans, projects, schedules. Establish a reflective mood. Sometimes it helps to take a few deep breaths with your eyes closed. Slowly roll your head and neck, lift your shoulders several times. Get rid of the tension. Picture yourself in a very pleasant, relaxing, peaceful spot: a place for reflection. A meadow of wildflowers swaying in the breeze. A mountaintop at sunrise. A deep quiet forest of barren pines. The seashore at summer's end—perhaps you are walking along as dusk falls. Can you remember a time and place where you felt very happy? Maybe that will be the setting you visualize. Take the minutes you need to create a vivid place with yourself fully present in it.

Taking Time for Reflecting

When you are ready, ask yourself the following questions and write down the answers.

1. What matters to me most in life?

. . . .

. . . .

. . . .

2. What is my destination?

. . . .

. . . .

. . . .

3. What baggage from the past is weighing me down?

. . . .

. . . .

. . . .

4. What obstacles lie in my path now?

. . . .

. . . .

. . . .

. . . .

5. Who matters most to me?

. . . .

. . . .

. . . .

Visualizing a Future of Time-Integration

Here's the time to take a mental journey, reviewing your life as a whole: the past you've emerged from, the present with its harried, driven, distracted atmosphere, and the future you would like to have. The vital, precious elements will of themselves appear vividly present, while other events, burdens, tasks, situations, relationships, will fade into the background. You will discover "clusters" in your life which are associated with pleasure, caring, pride; other "clusters"—which may be taking up great chunks of your time—will be associated with distaste, indifference, or strong rejection. You'll conclude that your time should belong to those people and tasks which bring satisfaction, substance, meaning to your life. You'll see it's time for a change.

Time Robbers

M. H. Luzatto wrote in *Mesillat Yesharim*, "Stealing time is also robbery." That statement written in 1740 is still true. Given the questions you've just answered, you now need to ask who or what is robbing you of your time, that which belongs to you. Time robbers fall into four categories. Ask yourself which one is robbing you the most of your time. Consider briefly for each category the amount of weekly time you think is fair to spend, then compare that to the amount of time you actually spend weekly.

Category	Hours I Should Give	Hours I Do Give
Job	_____	_____
Family	_____	_____
Friends	_____	_____
Chores	_____	_____
Myself	_____	_____
Other	_____	_____

Work out the percentages. Then, in each of the two circles below, distribute your time percentages in both categories, as if you're slicing pieces of a pie. This will help you visualize the differences between the way you feel you should spend your time and the way you actually do.

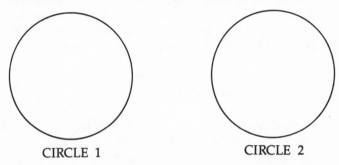

CIRCLE 1   CIRCLE 2

If you find that you can't give a fairly accurate estimate of the usual allotments of your time in an average week, then keep a chart for two weeks, or even three weeks, if your schedule varies considerably, to determine exactly how you spend your time. You may be surprised at your discoveries. When you have accurate information, you will be ready to begin remolding your life to the shape you want it to take.

Begin to Reclaim Your Hours

Now begins the task of reclaiming your time. Where are the areas in your life that you're giving inordinate amounts of time, that is, more time than you want to, more time than you feel you ought to, more time than the task should take or the person has a right to demand, more time than is reasonable. List them below.

1. _____

2. _____

3. _____

And now, what are the 3 areas in your life that you feel deserve more of your time? List them below.

1. _____

2. _____

3. _____

When you compare the two lists, you may be surprised to see a significant gap between how much you care and how much time you give to a specific person or activity. You may be chagrined to realize how very little time you spend with the people who matter most to you, and how much time on the relationships and responsibilities that matter the least, or bring you the least satisfaction. In chapters 10, 11, and 12, we will concentrate on your worklife and career. For now, let us focus on your self, your personal life, your relationship to loved ones.

Steal Back "Bytes" of Time for Yourself

Perhaps you've detected that you are your own worst enemy. You give time profligately to everybody and everything but yourself. Therefore, look to yourself first and foremost. This is not selfishness but a matter of self-esteem and, even more fundamentally, self-preservation. One of the women I interviewed, a successful college professor, recounted to me this story: "When I was raising my three children and had a difficult husband, I had a full-time teaching position while also working on a graduate degree. I kept taking up the slack for everybody until I finally felt I was left with no inner resources of my own. I had to start preserving myself."

Since you have segmented time into tiny "bytes" that extend over your entire week, your strategy initially must be to steal back small "bytes" for yourself every day. Reclaim some of the time of your life for pure play, pure enjoyment, pure pleasure. It doesn't have to be lots of time: nobody who suffers from Urgency Addiction would even consider that. Nor am I advising you to run away from any of your responsibilities. Not at all. Just be on the lookout for minutes you can steal for pleasure. This way you can reverse a habit which you may not even be aware you have acquired, which is to continually steal minutes for more work, more chores, more deals, more problems to worry about. Here are some suggestions:

- Select a day two weeks in advance and schedule lunch with a friend you haven't seen in six months or more.
- Spend 10 minutes on a park bench watching the passing scene.
- Pick a beautiful day and take a 15-minute stroll before starting your daily schedule.
- If you find yourself alone in an elevator, refuse to watch the numerals. Instead, take some deep breaths, roll your shoulders, relax!
- Call a friend (instead of a client) on your car phone just to have a brief chat.

- If you feel especially tired, pack it in and go to bed an hour earlier than usual. Sleep is a miraculous cure for mental as well as physical fatigue. As Shakespeare said, sleep "knits up the ravelled cares of time."
- Say "no" to the next person who makes an unreasonable demand on your time.
- If a meeting is canceled, play hooky and go browsing in nearby shops for an hour.
- Buy yourself something you want but don't need.
- Take your watch off for a whole Sunday.
- Allow yourself to do absolutely nothing for 5 minutes.
- Write a note to a friend you don't have time to see.

Add Pleasures to Your Daily Life

One of the habits you've fallen into as time pressures have gradually overwhelmed you is that of putting off pleasure, playtime, spontaneous enjoyments of the small things in life. You probably tell yourself dozens of times every day that you will take a day off just for fun sometime in the future. You'll take a leisurely lunch with a friend, let's say, when the current pressure is off. You'll take a *real* three-week vacation sometime within the next two years. What has happened is that you are gradually squeezing all spontaneous pleasure and enjoyment out of your life. In trimming the "fat" out of your daily schedule, you thought pleasure was dispensable.

After a while, you tend to forget what it feels like to be spontaneous. Acting on impulse becomes out of the question. You will censor yourself automatically. Playfulness will disappear from your personality. You will laugh less often, smile infrequently. Your conscious mind is saying, "I don't have time for that," but you are sending the message to your subconscious that says, "I don't deserve time for myself. I'm doing too many important things." Which is silly. What's more important than yourself?

Taking a Break from the Treadmill

Little things matter, too. These suggestions are the first baby steps you need to take. It would be too dizzy a leap to jump off the fast-moving time treadmill you're on. I understand that. Obligations and habits that have accumulated over a period of months or years can't be thrown over in a day. And you wouldn't want to do that. But you need relief *now*. When you start getting a little relief, you will start to yearn for more.

New habits will of themselves start to sprout. The point is to take what pleasure you can from whatever prospects lie within reach.

Remember what you once knew: how to enjoy the moment you're inhabiting. Not every activity has to have a goal. Not every moment must be productive. Let the activity itself, the pure enjoyment of it, be the goal. Pleasure, fun, play, joy, satisfaction, and enjoyment are great whenever they happen. Let them be!

During the period when I was greatly time-pressured, for example, I realized I had gotten out of shape and signed up for a fitness class twice a week. At first I could hardly keep up with the others. I huffed and puffed, tripped over my own feet, and felt exhausted 10 minutes into the hour. My body had even forgotten how to sweat. But I persisted in this torture. Slowly I improved, and added a third class with visions of all the things I would soon have the energy to do. Six months passed. I notched up to the next fitness level. At this point, since I could easily follow the instructor, I began to use this time to think through my problems, worry about my family's problems, make grocery lists, plan my work schedule for the next month, and so forth.

One day I walked out of class feeling bone tired. What good was this doing me? Then it dawned on me that I was using the hour of exercising just to heap worries and obligations on myself. I immediately decided to leave all that baggage at the gym door and enter fully into the exercise for the entire session. I would enjoy the pleasure of feeling my body in motion. Each hour of class would be *my time* and nobody else's. Now I almost always leave class refreshed and full of energy.

Our Own Time: It's All We've Got

Fight to get back your time, and then never give it up lightly again. Time-pressured people tend to live too much in the future or the past and to have too little regard for the present—an irony, since these same time-pressured people are busy packing the moment with everything they can find to put into it! In the meantime, big goals may get postponed indefinitely.

You Can't Have the Past Back

Nobody will give you back lost time for good behavior. Time belongs to you, but if you gave away to others time that was necessary for yourself, that time is gone forever. You can't have it back. But what you can do is take command of your time right now and resume ownership. Don't lose more time by regrets over the past.

Making Clock Time Your Own

There are times when we must live by the clock. But even that time belongs to you. You always have ownership of your time and need never give that up. You decide to "assign" some of your time to clock measurement. That's okay and necessary. Even during your clock-time activities, however, your awareness that you have chosen to measure this time by the clock will give you psychological mastery. But keep trying to add the other kind of time into your life: the time that allows you to express yourself without pressure, or even awareness of the passage of time. Wean yourself from overdependence on the clock. What's overdependence? A friend of mine found himself depressed when his beloved watch had to spend two weeks in the repair shop!

Of course you can get satisfaction out of clock time, too. I happen to have a zest for list-making (inherited straight from Cotton Mather I think!) and find it enjoyable to cross off items accomplished. It's a question of proportion and balance: my whole self is not reducible to the list of items to be acted on today.

Being Present to People Who Matter

None of us can have yesterday back, and tomorrow has not yet arrived, but todays belongs to you. The people who matter most to you should play some part in this day. I asked a number of successful people how they manage to integrate in a fulfilling way family and friends into their busy lives. One thing they all said was that they reduced the time spent with negative people, whether relatives or not.

Seven Ways to Connect with People Who Matter When You Don't Have Time for Anybody:

1. Write a short note instead of making a phone call. You can dash off in 5 minutes a letter that lasts forever, while the telephone can be a trap.
2. Go out to a casual restaurant impromptu with friends. Save cooking and cleanup time at home, plus the time it takes to get dressed up for a formal reservations-only restaurant.
3. Arrange something fun to do with friends well in advance, and put it on the calendar, just as you ordinarily do for important business dates.

4. Send flowers to a relative you love but can't spend time with right now.
5. Add up the time you spent watching television last night, and spend that same amount of time this evening on the phone with a loved one.
6. Award a small "time gift" to a friend or relative. Take a young child out for a treat. My sister Carol once took my three young children for a weekend, and it was worth more than gold to me.
7. A busy executive I interviewed keeps a well-worn Rolodex within reach on his desk—containing the names and numbers of friends all around the globe. Whenever he has a few spare minutes, he gives one of them a short call.

Mellow Time: Beatrice

How to make time for real friendships to grow and develop? My friend Beatrice told me how she has solved this problem. "The network of friendships today has shallow roots—people move, drop out, get involved in other things. You have to keep reaching out for replacements. Don't be the center of this network. Then people will look to you to be the leader, the organizer."

She described what she called "mellow time." "For me this is Friday nights. I tell a few of my close friends to drop over. We don't dress up. We eat and talk—nobody has to perform, everything is very relaxed.

"I am very aware of my own internal rhythms. I distinguish between existential time and clock time. Existential time is for myself and friends. If you're with your lover, time stands still. If you're doing something wonderful, time stretches out and seems to last forever. On the other hand, if you're waiting in an airport, a half hour can seem like ten hours."

She pointed out, however, that not every person who wants to take up your time should be accommodated. "You have to protect yourself from 'intruders'—these are people who call you up when it suits them, talk about the subjects that they want to talk about, will dump a lot of emotional sludge on you, then disappear until the next time they want to dump on you. I'm in touch with my existential time. I preserve myself when I feel it being used up too much."

The First Lady's View

When First Lady Barbara Bush spoke to the graduation class of Wellesley College in June 1990, she had this to say to them:

"As important as your obligations as a doctor, a lawyer, or a business leader may be, your human connections with spouses, with children, with friends, are the most important investment you will ever make."

Mrs. Bush went on, "At the end of your life, you will never regret not having passed one more test, not winning one more verdict or not closing one more deal. You will regret time not spent with a husband, a child, a friend, or a parent."

Surveys show that most Americans would agree with Mrs. Bush. But beliefs and actions are different. Besides, it's not as easy as it used to be. In the aftermath of World War II, the typical family consisted of father, the breadwinner; mother, the homemaker; and an average of four children. Now millions of American families with children consist of either two working parents or a single working parent. This means that, in the same 24-hour-day, one person must accomplish everything (and sometimes a great deal more) that was formerly divided up between two people.

Moreover, the extended family—grandparents, aunts and uncles, siblings, cousins, are much more scattered geographically and fragmented emotionally than even 20 years ago. With divorce occurring in one of every two marriages, there are complicated emotional and time demands related to custody and visitation rights, blending of duplicate "sets" of grandparents and mothers with step-mothers, and siblings with remarried spouses' children, and so on.

On top of that, time pressures weigh heavier on most of us because we aren't able to socialize with our extended family members in a way that used to be natural when they lived around the corner instead of 500 miles away. The time once given over to casual and intimate socializing now tends to get spent in longer work hours. That's why special effort must be made to spend time with people who matter.

Three Generations of Family Changes

My own family is typical of the sweeping social changes in American family life. When my parents got married and had their first baby in Chicago, both sets of their parents lived nearby. My parents lived in a duplex right around the corner from my mother's parents. Every morning my grandmother and one or another of my aunts came over to help—they had a lot of fun together amid ironing, bottle feeding, and taking the baby out in the stroller. By the time I got married and had my first baby, my husband and I lived in Pittsburgh, with both sets of our parents in distant cities. I had nobody around the corner to help me. Instead of calling my mother when the baby got sick, I consulted Dr. Spock. And the current generation of new mothers is primarily concerned with finding acceptable day care in the few weeks after the baby's birth before they have to go back to work.

Negotiating Time: Putting into Play What Matters

For people suffering from time urgency, there is never enough time. To put it another way, there are exceptionally large demands being made on your time. It is a real, not easily solvable problem. The skill you need to learn is how to make your time serve your purposes. You start with minutes and hours, and soon the days and weeks will follow. The process is not one of breaking time slots into tinier and tinier segments and squeezing more and more tasks into each slot. It is rather a new kind of effort at transforming your time. Your goal is to make the way you spend your time be a true reflection of who you are, what your goal in life is, and what matters to you the most.

The practical skill of negotiating time has two dimensions. The first is negotiating uses for time that can be agreed upon by yourself and others, usually those in your own household. In this sense, negotiating is a process of bargaining, arranging for and settling on uses for your time through discussion back and forth, with give and take on both sides.

The second dimension, which takes into account that the demands being made on your time are complicated and not easily dispensed with, is analogous to the way you might drive your car over difficult terrain, marked by hills and curves, and obstacles such as boulders and obscured views. In such a circumstance you would maneuver carefully, bringing all your skills and alert attention to bear, taking into consideration all the factors you could see. You would adjust your pace as the terrain suggested, moving around obstacles in some cases and speeding up in the clearings. In this sense, negotiating means being flexible and fluid, finding ways to use what time you have to reach the destination you desire.

In learning to negotiate time, you will become adroit at short-range plans and phased-in solutions; what's more, you will show a readiness to adapt to changing environments. Your sensitivity to time will enable you to keep your destination in mind despite the roadblocks in your path.

Household Chores Are Gender-Neutral Tasks

In Arlie Hochschild's study of working parents, *The Second Shift*, she found that many husbands and wives spend much valuable time and a great deal of emotional energy quarreling over the question of sex roles and marital roles. Whose job is it to take out the garbage? Paint the garage? Repair appliances? Take clothes to the dry cleaners? Vacuum the rug? Wash the dishes and make the beds?

She pointed out, "The happiest two-job marriages I saw were between men and women who did not load the former role of the housewife-mother onto the woman, and did not devalue it as one would a bygone 'peasant' way of life. They shared that role between them." She describes the "new man" as among those few who can discard outmoded notions of sexual role models and relate to women on a basis on equality.

My experience convinces me that we don't need to wait for an indeterminate future for things to get better between husbands and wives. In my interviews, I have found many "new men" eager to take on a fuller, more rounded and human role within the family. What I suggest below is a gender strategy which will allow you to save enormous amounts of needless time arguing over past divisions of labor which no longer make sense. The time for a better married life and family life is now.

The New Man and the New Woman: Personal Preferences Rather Than Gender-Dependent Tasks

The ways your parents divided the tasks of housekeeping and child-rearing between them are not relevant to your own situation. You will find, beneath many disagreements that occur over which partner should do which tasks, your own parents' marital disagreements. You need to break clear of that past and be free to construct your own home life. Start by listing on paper all the household tasks, indicating which of you usually does each one. Then sit down and negotiate a system, agreeing on two basic principles that could save loads of time and emotional energy.

1. Household tasks don't have gender tags on them. All household chores should be declared gender-neutral. This will free both husband and wife to parcel out the chores based on more practical considerations, such as who is available, who finds a given chore more or less palatable, or perhaps to set up a system of taking turns.

2. Everybody's time is intrinsically and equally valuable. Neither husband nor wife, mother nor daughter, father nor son, should claim that one person's time is more "sacred" than another's. This certainly should not be done based on the relative salaries of family members, which would use the formula "time is money" to diminish a loved one's human dignity.

Parenting Tasks Are Gender-Specific

Child care should not be lumped in with housekeeping chores. A house is just a house, a child is flesh of your flesh, a pearl beyond price. A baby's cry deserves more attention than windows in need of washing. These are statements so obvious as to be trite except, in time-driven households I have seen so often, the needs of children become simply more irksome items on the "must-do" list. Not that parents *feel* this way. It is rather that severe time urgency forces the most loving people into unnatural modes of behavior. Therefore, never put housekeeping tasks on the same list as child-care needs. They inhabit two different universes.

The gender question is just the opposite here. It doesn't matter to the rug whether it is vacuumed by a man or a woman, but to a child, both the mother and father matter tremendously, and each person knows how to be a father or a mother in a unique way. In agrarian times, the father was with the children as much as the mother; factories and high technology brought about the separation of the father, and now both parents, from the children's daily lives. Just as mothers are struggling to juggle jobs and motherhood, there are good signs that men want to be personally involved with their children again on a deep emotional level.

Two negotiating principles should be agreed upon by mothers and fathers:

1. Mothers and fathers are equally responsible for and needed by their children.
2. Each mother and each father has a deeply personal, unique way of expressing parental love, which should be respected.

Stephanie and Steve: Plight of Working Parents

Stephanie and Steve, the time-beleaguered couple we've already met, filled out their charts separately, then sat down to compare notes. They were astonished to see that at the top of both their lists was the goal: "Have a second baby." Each of them had privately thought it was impossible, given their time pressures, and had been afraid to confide in the other. As a result of their talk, they decided to find a way to proceed with a second pregnancy. They realized that until the decision to have a baby was made, they couldn't work out the practical problems of *how* to manage it.

The second issue that rose to the surface as they began to have conversations was the need for personal time. Stephanie's personal time has been "lost" and had to be found by both of them. Steve hadn't realized how severely deprived Stephanie felt, particularly since the birth of their first child. He agreed to turn over—as a sacrifice, really—half of the personal time he enjoyed, to his wife. Especially since they both wanted a second baby, Steve recognized that he needed to put more of his leisure time into parenting so that Stephanie could have back a sense of herself as a person.

Wayne and Sharon: She Goes Back to Work

Wayne and Sharon have worked out their solutions from a deep common understanding of who they are and where they're going. For this couple, marriage and family are paramount. When Wayne thought he had a secure, long-range future at Sears, he and Sharon planned that she would be a full-time mother until their two children reached high school age. They could afford for Sharon not to work outside the home, and both of them felt their lives were more fulfilling and less stressful with that arrangement. Sharon enjoyed homemaking, community affairs, involvement in an intensely personal way with her girls.

As the children progressed through grade school, Sharon was planning to enroll at Northwestern University for a graduate degree in communications. Going at a leisurely pace, she figured she would be reentering the workforce with a new career at about the time the girls were entering high school.

The Sears shake-up forced them to reevaluate. Wayne's economic future was now threatened. After many discussions, they concluded that planning for his future would be difficult. As the major breadwinner, he found himself in the vulnerable slot of middle management. To simply change companies, as so many others had done, would be possibly jumping from the frying pan into the fire.

In the short term, Sharon had greater flexibility and more options. They agreed to speed up her time line for going back to work. Sharon reconsidered her goals. Along with communications, she had always enjoyed the corporate climate and was interested in the revolutionized technological environment. She took a computer course at a nearby community college to update her skills and get current references from her professors, and within three months she had a half-time job at a nearby corporation. Without much strain on their all-important family life, she is positioning herself for advancement, and getting acclimated to the fluid corporate culture.

Both Wayne and Sharon view this as an interim decision, and neither one of them expects it to provide a long-term solution. But they have taken back their own time. The reins are in their hands now. They have moved out of the paralyzing panic-ridden stage. Although Sharon's income is no substitute for Wayne's, if he were suddenly fired, he would get a severance package, and she would be already back in the workforce with current skills and contacts. Sharon is using every minute on the job to learn more skills which will stand her in good stead in the future. They have, moreover, reallocated their household chores—Wayne does more to help, having decided not to put in crazy work hours as a knee-jerk response to job pressures. Their strategy is sound. They are buying time to make long-range plans.

Ann-Marie: Weighed Down by Past Baggage

Ann-Marie, the traveling bank auditor, was initially very frightened when she felt her marriage was falling into a pattern of inequality where she would be relegated to all the household chores while her husband got all the leisure time. Once she got past these fears, through frank conversations and negotiations with Felix, she realized that she had been allowing baggage from her past—her parents' marriage—to get in the way. In times of stress, we all tend to regress to the past. What rose up in Ann-Marie's memory, blocking her usually rational planning, was the picture of her father ruling the roost as her mother slaved to satisfy his every whim.

When Felix began his graduate studies, he proposed that she take over the household chores for the duration—believing this was a fair and temporary arrangement. Ann-Marie agreed, but resentfully: He was spending time to get a degree that he deeply desired, but why should she have to pay for it by having her private time taken up with extra work?

Finally, realizing that Felix was not her father, she broached the topic with him and was surprised to find him immediately contrite. He accused himself of selfishness, saying he assumed she was having a glamorous time on the road and didn't mind spending weekends doing household chores and laundry.

"As I spoke," Felix said, grinning sheepishly, "I saw how insensitive I sounded. Why would anybody think it was fun to do laundry?"

They decided to hire help. Here again, Ann-Marie's past weighed her down. Felix made this suggestion, which she rejected at first because her father would have disapproved. Yet her marriage, as Felix reminded her, was different. They both had good incomes and felt that the expense was justified in order to give them both the time they wanted. They got housecleaning help once a week and found a high school student with a car to run errands on Saturday mornings. This would not be a solution for everybody, but it worked for them—at this stage of their lives. They evaluated their time based on who they were and where they were going.

Preserving precious leisure time was more important than the speed at which their savings mounted.

Jason and His Parents: Negotiating Compromises

The most serious dilemma, and perhaps the most common one, is the conflict between two things of equal importance. What Jason the newspaper editor came to see was that two things which mattered greatly to him, his career and his parents, were creating tangled time lines in his life. A series of compromises were finally negotiated. He met with his rabbi, who put him in contact with various community organizations that could offer him support and advice. There were many thousands of young professionals, said the rabbi, who faced and overcame these problems. He was not the first.

Jason finally worked out a complex solution which involved some paid help, some volunteer help through his temple and community association, and better organization of his own time. He went into short-term counseling, which helped him realize that he was dealing with a sudden overwhelming problem that could nevertheless be handled. Sometimes there are temporary time jam-ups that can be worked out rationally. He learned to prevent panic from turning him into a victim himself. He got better focused for his future.

Quantitative vs. Qualitative Time

If we live always and only by the clock, we never experience the deeply satisfying dimension of time which puts us in touch with our life as a whole. Clock time is quantitative time: little intervals to be filled up with productivity. But there is time beyond the clock, which we may call qualitative time. To have a significant human life, we must recognize and accept, embrace even, these qualities of time when they present themselves: endurance, flow, duration, intensity, joy, ecstasy, happiness, trust, deep truth. When such moments occur, you must drop everything and live that time. You need to get past the harried condition of always being trapped in quantitative time—segmented activity. You need to focus on who you are and what your destination is. In the next chapter you will learn how to balance quantitative and qualitative time. You will find a self-nurturant program to put you in touch with your deepest self.

9
FINDING YOUR OWN PACE: RECLAIMING YOURSELF

There's no clock in the forest.

—SHAKESPEARE, *AS YOU LIKE IT*

People who give up personal time believe at first that they are dispensing with leisure for a brief period. As the weeks slip into months, the absence of private time that belongs to nobody else begins to seem natural. Finally, only a vague feeling of loss remains, signalling serious damage to self-esteem. Last to go is the sense of self—that deeper awareness of one's unique identity.

The very people who demonstrate outstanding performance to the world often display poor judgment regarding their own deep personal needs. They resist reclaiming themselves. Despite persistent anguish, they vehemently reject any suggestion that they take time for themselves. They may be secretly convinced they don't deserve personal time, although their public claim will be that they don't desire it. The loss of self deepens. Emotional numbness sets in.

If you've read this far in the book, you know that it's time to reclaim yourself. In taking back the time that belongs to you, you will recover your self-esteem and a confident sense of who you are. Your freedom will emerge in all its glory.

I know your time is precious. I know minutes are gold coins. I know you think you don't have time for yourself. But keep reading. Stick to the path a little longer. This way lies freedom.

Most of us are so dependent on clock time that we forget there's another kind of time which belongs to us in a cozy and intimate way. This kind of time—lodged within our bodies and natural to our minds and hearts—has its origins in a primordial past long before a set of gears on the wall told us when to go to bed. Getting back in touch with the time inside yourself will be a powerful aid to reclaiming yourself.

123

Timing Is in Our Genes

Timing is in our genes. We have reached a point in the late twentieth century when our daily routine seems to be entirely independent of nature—we can live a 24-hour indoor existence surrounded by the inventions of technology without ever seeing the light of day for months on end. But at this very point, the new science of chronobiology has arisen, demonstrating our intimate synchronization with nature's time. Scientists now have shown that our bodies are governed by cycles as ancient as life itself. At the center is the sun. Timing that is specifically tied to the rise and set of the sun every 24 hours—circadian rhythms, they're called—is embedded in our genes and guides the movements of our bodies in myriad and intricate ways. Through these circadian rhythms we are joined to just about every creature on the planet: a biological clock ticks away not only in us, but in every living thing.

The invention of the clock did not free us from the natural circadian rhythms within us, although the inventions of technology have diminished our ability to hear the harmony at work inside us. Now, as one circadian specialist remarked, we need to "create a new harmony between the time in our body and the time on our wrists."

The New Chronobiology

Chronobiology is a new science, based on observations that the human body operates according to set rhythms that are roughly synchronized to the 24-hour, light/dark, solar day. University of Minnesota researcher Franz Halberg took note of this fact 30 years ago, and coined the term, *circadian*, which combines two Latin words: *circa* (about), and *dies* (a day).

In 1972, French geologist Michele Cifra lowered himself for 6 months into a deep cave in Texas, where he lived isolated from the sun and all reminders of the passing of time. He kept to a strict routine, recording his body's natural rhythms, rode a stationary bike 3 miles, took his blood pressure, pulse readings, temperature, and heart rate. He phoned colleagues on the surface when he went to bed or ate a meal. This experiment proved that the natural human day is close to 25 hours long, and that every vital function has its own daily rhythm, which we notice only when the timing is off.

In 1989, an Italian woman, Stefania Follini, descended for 130 days into a cave in New Mexico, matching the conditions of her French predecessor, and expanding knowledge of our circadian rhythms.

Meanwhile, university researchers around the country have been working with fruit flies and hamsters to discover the physiology of circadian rhythms. Scientists at the University of Virginia in 1988, studying a mutant hamster, discovered a key cluster of nerve cells, called the suprachiasmatic nucleus (SCN), which is one-third of a millimeter in size and located in the hypothalamus, one of the older parts of the brain. SCN is a central body clock, which has led scientists to speculate that humans have it too. It is responsible for making us sleepy at night, alert during the day, and sets a beat for kidney, heart, lungs, and other organs, although some functions seem to have separate clocks, such as the adrenal glands.

Dr. Martin Moore-Ede, circadian physiologist and an associate professor at the Harvard Medical School, has established the Institute for Circadian Physiology in Boston. The Human Alertness Research Center has a lab set up there to probe and solve circadian disorders involving jet lag, sleep problems, depression, and difficulties faced by shift workers.

Listen to Your Internal Clock

For most of our time on earth, our internal circadian rhythms functioned beautifully. Our internal time kept harmony with external time. Before cars and trains and planes were invented, we could go only as fast as our horses could gallop. The pace of life in agrarian times was tied to the rise and fall of the sun, just as our bodies are. Our biological clock had little need for adjustments. But with the invention of the light bulb by Thomas Edison in 1883, followed by the swift growth of many forms of technology, we left our body clocks way behind us.

We became people of the night, a society with a 24-hour day in which every second counts. More than 20 million Americans work schedules that shift between day and night. Technology has given us the freedom to step out of synch with nature's rhythms, but it has also deprived us of an intimate sense of ourselves. The speedy pace of life has caused a war between our biological and our mechanical clocks.

Some chronobiologists speculate that we also function according to a number of weekly rhythms. These would govern changes in body chemicals, heartbeat and blood circulation, and the immune system. In fact, these rhythms may have something to do with the seven-day week as a unit of time—the only calendar unit that did not originate in astronomy.

What has happened to those of us who suffer from excessive time pressures is that we have gotten so harried by the constant pressure from the clock on the wall that we no longer listen to the natural clock inside our bodies.

Now it is time to change that. Not that we would want to get rid of our mechanical clocks or any of our technology. But we need also to let our natural rhythms assert themselves. They are a deeply necessary part of ourselves. We stifle them at too great a cost.

In this chapter you will learn how to listen to your internal clock. Tuning into your natural rhythms will be a powerful method for getting back in touch with yourself. You will find how to fine-tune your internal clock to what suits you best. You will discover your own pace and how to live in accordance with it.

The Body's Timing

In a fascinating book, *The Body in Time* (John Wiley & Sons, Inc., 1988), author Kenneth Jon Rose traces the numerous ways in which every part and function of our human selves is timed, with its own rhythms, from the conception and birth of an infant to the heartbeats, breathing, speaking, hiccuping, movements of the adult. "The marriage of the human body to the sun is an intimate and binding contract, one that is obeyed by the body in sickness as well as in health," he writes.

Our bodies are analogous to a symphony of rhythms. An internal pacemaker, or several of them, orchestrates our daily cycles. The key indicator of body time is the internal temperature, which rises and falls throughout the day rather than remaining at a constant 98.6 degrees. From a high of about 99.0 degrees at 6 in the evening, it gradually drops to a low of 97.0 degrees by 4 in the morning as dawn approaches. Our heartbeat may vary by as much as 20 to 30 beats per minute over a 24-hour stretch. Hormone levels fluctuate. Mood and memory swing up and down. Muscle contraction varies throughout the day. A handgrip, for instance, is strongest around 6:00 P.M. and weakest at 3:00 A.M.

So, too, sleep and wakefulness alternate with the regularity of the tides. The cells comprising the inner lining of the skin and digestive tract speed up their metabolic activity around midnight, only to slow down during the height of the day. Normal rhythmic cell activity is so predictable that it can be used to diagnose abnormal functions in the body. Enzymes that break down toxins and drugs are at their speediest around 2 A.M. and at their slowest at about 2 P.M. Virtually *every* body function shows a circadian rhythm, which is controlled internally but reset every 24 hours to mesh with the natural light of day.

The following four steps will put you back in touch with yourself, and will be the means to finding your own pace. It's a self-nurturing program that will bring you comfort right away, and eventually freedom.

Step 1: Spend Time with a Lost Friend: Nature

Go out to the wilderness whenever you can. Look for the niche in nature that feels right to you. Just as you slowly lost a sense of natural time over a period of years—or if you were an urban child maybe never experienced it—you will not reclaim it on a single Sunday jaunt to the nearest park.

Experiencing wilderness is crucial. If you choose a luxurious resort equipped with the appurtenances of hi-tech telecommunications—TV, VCR, phones, clocks, fax machines, dictaphones, and so forth, you may as well stay at the office. Better to enjoy several afternoon drives in the country than a weekend "getaway" where you bring everything along that keeps you hopping to clocks. Take from nature its eternally renewing energy, but also its stillness.

You can tell when nature is having the desired effect. Time pressures will ease away. The urge to check your watch will start to dissipate. Sleep under the stars and wake up by sunlight—both literally and figuratively. This experience will evoke a sense of belonging to an order of things that you can trust. You'll want to build on this trust; think of it as a healthful antidote to the pervasive attitude of distrust underlying our intensely competitive society.

Spending time with nature is a time-proven antidote for those obsessed with clocks, watches, schedules, lists, calendars, appointment books, deadlines—all the visible signs of human "mechanical time." In the wilderness you'll encounter a natural time humming to age-old rhythms: sunrise, sunset, the moon and tides, the seasons, the cycles of birth and eventual rebirth. The birds soaring overhead, the squirrels underfoot, the acorns and pine needles in the forest—all operate by the natural time that guides us too.

Don't forget: we also belong to the kingdom of nature. Only in the twentieth century, especially in the last few decades, have we forgotten what all the peoples of the earth before us took for granted.

I'm not urging you to become a flower child, 1960s-style. I'm not suggesting that you drop out of society. Not at all. I personally believe that, all things considered, this is the best time of all ages to inhabit our universe. But go to a place as much into wilderness as possible. Go often—maybe only a day every month or so if that is all you can manage. Revitalize yourself completely. Free yourself from the tyranny of the clock. Let nature have its way with you. Here's one account to whet your appetite.

Canoe Camping

"Imagine a day without telephones, cars, newspapers, or television; a week where money means nothing; two weeks without caring to know more about the time than the sun can tell you. Now place your unharried self on a peninsula that juts out into a corner of an uninhabited lake a two-day trip from the nearest road."

So begins an account by Pamela Monk, a middle school teacher in Ithaca, New York, writing about her wilderness experiences for *The New York Times* (June 24, 1990). She continues, "Each summer, for the past several years, my husband and I have taken our two children on an extended canoe camp. We began with lakes near Rollins Pond State Campground, in the Adirondacks, about 15 miles west of Saranac Lake, where it is possible to park a car on the shore of a lake and canoe to isolated campsites. We gradually increased the length of our stays until last year we managed a full 14 nights out in the wilds of Quetico Provincial Park in Ontario near the Minnesota border."

Monk describes canoe camping as a wilderness sport that includes backpacking and boating. It gives you the thrill of taking a journey through breathtakingly beautiful country "in one of the least intrusive vehicles ever designed by humans: the canoe."

She describes the marshy bay where moose come to feed at dawn, the inviting waterfall, the lazy afternoon fishing and swimming, or napping in a hammock strung between two pines. As the sun goes down, you build a fire to ward off the evening chill. In the gathering dusk, loons call to each other. A beaver swims by; the stars come out.

This is but one of a thousand variations possible for those who want a trek in the wilderness canoe parks found in abundance in Canada and the northeastern United States. Monk recommends as an excellent place for beginners the state campground at Rollins Pond in the St. Regis section of the Adirondack Forest Preserve. Canoes can be rented there by the day and you can start out with simple day trips that are not strenuous.

The Urban Wilderness for City People

Your connection with nature doesn't have to be so arduous. It can be as simple and uncomplicated as taking a stroll in the country. You may count yourself among the 75,000 people or more who belong to the urban trail movement. In dozens of states from Oregon to Maryland, people are speaking up with a vision of the future that includes natural trails and green spaces in the cities. People who want to walk and bike in the city have banded together to build walkways in old railroads beds and to construct paths that start in congested downtown areas and lead to distant farmlands.

Supporters of the urban trail movement say many of the transportation problems of big cities could be solved by bicycle commuters moving to work along the new trails. In Seattle, Washington, for example, thousands of bikers commute to their jobs along the Burke-Gilman Trail, a paved-over rail line. In Washington, D.C., the Chesapeake & Ohio Canal has attracted many walkers and bikers going to work. In Portland, one of the most popular areas is Tom McCall Waterfront Park, a grass and bike trail.

Look around your own community. Perhaps you can find an inviting urban trail. Within the next decade there may be a path blazed that would connect every city in America—leading through woods and dales, through the lights and excitement of center cities to the peacefulness of the country—and back again.

A Future of Greenways

With nearly 80 percent of the U.S. population now living in cities and towns, people across the nation are rising up to reactivate their love of nature. The President's Commission on Americans Outdoors (PCAO), appointed by Ronald Reagan in 1985, brought the word "greenway" into common usage and spread the trail-and-corridor-making fever. Greenways are corridors that link open spaces and bring an increasingly urbanized population to the outdoors. "We can tie this country together with threads of green that everywhere grant us access to the natural world," the commission report read. There are now about 250 greenways converted from railroad beds nationally. Demographics point to greenways as the paths of the future. Maryland Governor William Donald Schaefer recently appointed the first state commission of developers, environmentalists, and government officials to launch a statewide greenways program.

"The word is really a combination of 'greenbelt' and 'parkway,' taking the better part of each," says Charles E. Little, author of a forthcoming book on the subject. "I estimate about 500 individual projects are under way in the U.S." Advocates of greenways envision a national interconnected system of paths. "A four-year-old organization called the Rails-to-Trails Conservancy is working towards that end. Of perhaps 150,000 total miles of rail lines abandoned so far, some 3,100 miles in 35 states have become trails."—Noel Grove, "Greenways: Paths to the Future," *National Geographic,* June 1990

Step 2: Exercise for Self-Discovery

We Americans know the benefits of exercise for health and fitness. Of the many forms of exercise, however, you want to take up the kind of exercise especially designed to restore a sense of vital self-awareness, a feeling of belonging to one's body. These feelings have gotten buried, if not lost, in the furious race against time that you've been running. Competitive exercise—whether against others or yourself—is not the point. Your goal is not to win or to punish or to overcome. What you're after is a rhythmic, focused body movement which rewards you with a heightened awareness of your body, and thus yourself. Think about the kind of movement which you enjoy for its own sake—walking, stretching, or perhaps dancing. It's not what you do—how strenuous or how great the skills you employ—but rather what it does for you, what suits you and gives you the most natural satisfaction.

You may want to consider one of the many variations of yoga. Increasingly, as a result of research in the field of sports medicine, athletes are being trained according to such modes of gentle, rhythmic, focused movements; the goal is self-empowerment through micro-movements. Among them, let me mention Krepalu Yoga, based in Lenox, Massachusetts, which is a form of meditation in motion. "Listen to the body. It will tell you what it wants," says yoga instructor Sharon Rudolph. "The approach we take is to follow the body's lead. Go with what feels right for you. There are no rules, no endurance tests to perform." The object is not to sweat and grunt, but to engage in bodily movement that brings you the calmness, the intensity, the satisfaction of being totally present in the *now*. You are giving your body a regular, well-deserved treat.

Sunrise Pleasures

Many people report that they combine the pleasures of nature with the satisfaction of exercise. Marguerite, a graduate student in Claremont, California, studying for her doctoral exams, says she loves to rise with the sun and take a drive to the nearby mountains, where she then gets out of the car and goes for an invigorating jog before she starts a day of intense academic preparation. She enjoys the feeling of stretching her body and feeling its movement in the early morning air. It helps her clear her mind for the day's work. In California she has a lot of company. The beaches of Malibu are welcoming to many surfers who arrive before sunrise, when the breezes are mild and the water's surface silky.

Getting a Sense of the Present

Whether or not the exercise takes place in a wilderness environment or near the seashore or in mountains, or in a sweaty gym, or the privacy of your own bedroom, the point is to put you in touch with yourself. Jon Kabat-Zinn, Ph.D., associate professor of preventive and behavioral medicine at the University of Massachusetts School of Medicine at Worcester, says in an article from *Self*, "Pay attention to the rhythm of your breathing, or the feeling of your footfall, step after step, or the sense of trees passing, or the feeling of air on your skin—anything at all as long as you are doing it on purpose. The more you actually practice paying attention in systematic ways and use your mind while exercising, the more frequently you will have those experiences [of bringing your mind closer to the actuality of your moment-to-moment experience] and the deeper it will be."

Through this kind of noncompetitive exercise, you will be trying to reintegrate time as a natural flow in your daily life. The "place" where this sense of flow happens is in the present. Thus, in restoring an awareness of your self experiencing that present, you are recapturing a true sense of time. The effect is to relieve the heavy burden of time pressure at your back. You will recover the moment as the place where time "collects" itself in its integrity. Thereby a sense of wholeness envelops you. The satisfaction and pleasure are derived from the experience of the activity for its own sake.

Swimming a Ritual Mile

Sara Rimer, a reporter for *The New York Times*, finds a sense of wholeness and a meditative pleasure from swimming in an indoor pool. She described in a 1990 article how she regularly swims a ritual mile, counts laps, sings the same songs to herself. She explains, "The counting is a kind of meditation, an aquatic metronome that drives out all the internal flotsam. I leave the pool with a sense of well-being that carries me through the day." And for an urban dweller, she writes, the swimming pool can be a special refuge—where water blocks out the psyche-jarring noises of traffic and human commotion.

Connecting Up with the Past

For many people, I suspect, a favorite sport or physical activity is tied to good childhood memories, bringing with it a sense of time-integration, a sense of the flow of the person through life. For me this has always been horseback riding, an engrossing childhood experience. Driving through the countryside today, if I see a field of horses grazing, it fills me with nostalgic pleasure. For others it might be family volleyball games or woodland hikes.

For Sara Rimer, swimming also has this memory-laden dimension. She recounts in her article that she learned to swim at around 5 years old and joined a swim team at 8 years, continuing through high school with swim meets almost every weekend. She recalls, "My mother, who did not have the opportunity to learn to swim when she was a child, made my swimming childhood possible. She drove me to the pool, and she urged me on. In the pool now, I still hear the sound of the coach's whistle at practice, the starting gun at meets, the crowd cheering. Now, more than ever, I count on swimming for a sense of order."

Step 3: Meditate

Meditation is simply listening to yourself. It is nothing to fear. One of the traits I've noticed from the beginning in people haunted by time pressures is their lack of focus, a certain harried distracted appearance. You never feel that this person is totally with you; that is usually because he or she is thinking of the list of things to finish doing. They may have darting eyes, check their watches, shift their bodily position often, and so on. Time—rather than the conversation of the moment—is on their minds. Creativity and spontaneous pleasure spring from the deep wells within ourselves. The need to have a strong, sure sense of yourself is primary if you suffer from time urgency. I don't like to use the word "meditation" because it sounds esoteric to many busy, success-oriented people—as if it were a dropout program for flower children of a previous generation. Not at all.

Sit quietly for five minutes each day—don't tell me you can't find five minutes!—in order to restore yourself to a natural sense of time. Instead of being driven by a sense of time urgency, you want to regain self-assurance. You desire to be no longer harried by outside forces, but to be directed from within the core of your own personality. Be still for a few minutes each day to let your own voice speak to you. Time-driven people squash the sound of their inner selves. It is better to start out with frequent short sessions rather than lengthy but infrequent meditations. You will make greater progress that way.

Is There a Special Method for Meditation?

The object of listening to yourself, which is the basis for meditation, is to regain a sense of mastery over your life. As you learn to listen to your deeper self, you'll trust your ability to flow with your own individual temperament. The idea is not to retreat from society and the world, to hole up in a remote shack somewhere. Rather it is to look inside yourself in order to reformulate your sense of who you are and to get time back in your life in a natural way. Instead of being enslaved by time urgency, you want to regain a sense of ease and freedom. You desire to be no longer at the mercy of outside forces.

The first few times you meditate, your mind may be full of static. The internal motor is running on high. It may be impossible to shut out the distracting images that flit in and out of your brain, like bees buzzing, or flies swarming around you. So get a method. Any method will do, as long as it appeals to you. Bookstores are stocked with videos and audios that will give you a program—everything from soft music to the sounds of nature to a yoga reading. Whatever suits you is fine. But stay with it. You will soon be agreeably surprised that your mind quiets down, becomes receptive, calm, and ready for the experience. Then you will easily descend into the core of your self, where the balance, the center, the sense of being at one with the flow of time awaits you. All meditation programs, both from the East and the West, share the basic goal of helping you get in tune with the ultimate order in the universe—though language and belief patterns differ greatly on the surface.

Zen on the Lawn

Jennifer Pearce, my exercise instructor, told me about a wonderful course she took in college which combined Eastern and Western spirituality: Zen taught by a Jesuit priest, Dr. Ben Wren. The class meditated in a large empty room that served as office and classroom for Father Wren. With shoes removed, they sat on the floor in the cross-legged lotus posture. Outdoors they danced T'ai Chi, a type of meditation in motion, on the quadrangle of Loyola University in New Orleans, performed to music amplified by loudspeakers. The dances were so beautiful and graceful that tourists would often hop off the sight-seeing trolleys that passed by the quad and stay to watch for a while; they apparently regarded the Zen dancing as part of the sights. Jennifer told me she was puzzled at first by the seeming contradiction of a Western priest teaching a course in Eastern philosophy. Yet the merging of nature, exercise, and meditation brought her a tremendous sense of peace and self-possession which has remained with her long after most of her college courses have been forgotten.

Stephanie's Hideaway

I can't reassure you enough that meditation is natural and easy. Stephanie was reluctant when I first suggested it to her, but she and Steve were agreed that she had to have some regular personal time to herself before they embarked on the next pregnancy. As a new mother, she used to pop awake early every morning to listen for the baby's first whimper and at the same time review obsessively the long list of things to be done that day. That meant she often started the day with dread.

At my suggestion she made one small change. Now she slips out of bed (she also goes to bed an hour earlier most evenings) and moves into a tiny bedroom down the hall which she has converted into a hideaway; it's not much bigger than a closet, but all her own, with pretty things that appeal to her. She sinks into an old gingham-covered armchair given to her by her grandmother, filled with homey associations, and closes her eyes. She rests her hands, palms up, in her lap, does a few shoulder and neck rolls to relax, and closes her eyes. Then she takes three or four deep breaths, and goes down into herself, where she simply listens to her inner voice. She says this practice has given her a whole new sense of herself. Her daily "to-do" list has changed. On the old list, everything was a "must-do." Now the true "must-dos" have shrunk in number, with many items mentally labeled "would like to do," and a few relegated to the pile headed: "Forget it—life's too short."

Step 4: Welcome Unmanaged Time

Just as nature needs renewal, so do you. If you suffer from time urgency, unmanaged time may be greeted with panic. But it is essential to recapture the ability to enjoy unstructured time—which you probably regard as wasting time. What I'm talking about, the Italians have a phrase for. It's called "dolce far niente"—which, roughly translated means "it's great to do absolutely nothing." Before you can enjoy unmanaged time, you must learn to trust yourself. What kind of trust? Trust that if you relax a bit, you won't drop out, become a failure. Stop monitoring yourself. You have gotten so used to managing every minute of your time that you will now have to teach yourself to recognize a chance for "unmanaged" time and to take it—exuberantly.

Brief Pleasures, Valid Escapes

People who suffer from time urgency usually feel that they have to make the maximum of every moment in order to meet all their tasks and obligations. As part of the overall self-care plan, you need to readjust your thinking so that you regard odds-and-ends of time as found opportunities to nurture yourself by doing what you want to do rather than what you must do. It's part of taking back ownership of your own time. Since you have segmented your time into tiny modules that extend across your entire day, your nights, months, seasons, your very life—the strategy in Step 4 is to steal back small moments for yourself. You need to retrain yourself to find pockets of time that haven't been filled, or to learn how to "catch" yourself in an idle period and use it for enjoyment.

Reclaim some of the time of your life for pure play, pure enjoyment, pure pleasure. This is not to suggest that you take a lot of time for yourself every day—nobody suffering from time urgency would even consider such a possibility. All I am saying is this: be on the lookout for minutes you can steal for pleasure. You can pick up some of the suggestions below, but within a few weeks you will find yourself picking out little activities you can fit into your day without sacrificing any essential commitments.

Give yourself a pat on the back for every pleasure module you squeeze in. It will seem artificial at first. Don't worry. What starts out mechanically can flow into a natural, organic experience. Spontaneity will bubble back into your life.

Step 4 is the *opposite* of time management. Its purpose is to teach you not to panic at a little open space of unscheduled time, but to enjoy it.

I asked 25 very busy, successful people what they do when the pace gets too frantic. Here are some of their favorites:

Beatrice: If I can't get out to nature, I bring it home. I stop at the supermarket, get a bunch of flowers, come home and arrange them. It relaxes me.

Nancy: I go to a lecture on some subject I'm totally unfamiliar with.

Mary Ann: I put a birdbath and feeder in my backyard instead of a garden. Now I love to sit on the porch and watch the birds whenever I can steal a few minutes.

Allison: I send my husband and three kids to a Saturday afternoon movie and soak up absolute peace and quiet.

Jon: I take off my watch on Friday night and don't put it back on till Monday morning.

Tona: I read a travel magazine and dream.

Catherine: I read a cookbook—don't make anything, just read it.

Al: Go to a movie. Great escape!

Sandra: Curl up in bed with a trashy novel.

Marge: Get the latest exercise video and do it.

Ted: I get up before dawn and go deer hunting with my father and brother.

Lee: Get a professional massage.

Susan: Throw away all unloved, dowdy clothes.

Jim: Get up 15 minutes earlier to read the morning newspaper in peace.

Alan: Turn off the phone.

Phyllis: I get my nails done.

Ed: Plan a lobster lunch with my wife, browse in used bookstores.

Elizabeth: Call up and cancel an obligation I foolishly agreed to.

Dan: Go for a walk.

It Takes Time to Find Your Own Pace

Don't be rushed. Don't get impatient. You did not fall victim to Urgency Addiction overnight. Rather you succumbed gradually to the pressures of the external environment—friends and associates, your boss, corporate rules, the unspoken messages of requirements for success—by stepping up your pace. You also answered the internal call of your own desire for achievement, recognition, and success. You found yourself on a treadmill that began to go faster and faster until one day you realized that time had become a constant preoccupation, a tyrant ruling your life. There's a chasm separating your apparent self—assured, in control of every situation, a world-class super-achiever—and your inner self—emotionally exhausted, driven, harried, deprived of every satisfaction.

What lies in your future is freedom. Perhaps in the past you have yearned to get free of the burden of this nearly unbearable time urgency, but hesitated to take the steps you felt were necessary. You feared you would have to give up too much. You feared that the price would be too high: failure—or almost as bad—a lower rung of the career ladder, the slow track, the place relegated to the almost-made-its. Not true. All you have to lose is the pain you carry, mostly hidden from those around you.

The program you are embarking on should not be considered a short-term effort for getting over a small hump. It is a path to freedom for the rest of your life. To get back in synchronization with time is to recapture your true self. Recognize that growth involves ups and downs. Realize that at first you will be swimming upstream most of the time. Look for milestones along the way. Accept partial solutions.

In order to become a time-integrated person, you need to take all the steps. Tend to every area of your life—career, personal time, relationships, your own self-nurturing activities. Only a total effort will produce a reversal of Urgency Addiction. You entered a door which led you away from your true relation to time. Now you are on your way back to that same door. You'll open it and step outside to the place where you belong. Give yourself time.

Review the Steps

1. Realize that time belongs to you.
2. Learn from the traits of time-integrated people.
3. Recognize that there's time enough for everything that matters, then decide what matters.
4. Spend time with a lost friend: Nature.
5. Exercise for self-discovery.
6. Get centered through meditation.
7. Welcome unmanaged time for yourself.
8. Give yourself time to find your own pace.

Taking Back Ownership of Your Work Time

10

THE CORPORATE CLOCK: RUNNING ON GLOBAL TIME

Nothing is ours, except time.

—SENECA, A.D. 65

You have embarked on a strong personal program to reclaim your time and yourself. You should soon begin to feel renewed vigor and creativity. But if you're like most Americans, the central focus of your problem with time pressure is your job. That is where you feel the greatest time demands and where you feel most vulnerable, least free to make changes. But you should not worry, because that is the issue we are taking up for this final section of the book. In these last three chapters, you will learn how to take back ownership of your work time.

My goal is to help you to not merely survive but to flourish in the totally transformed work environment we all inhabit. As the decade of the 1990s rushes headlong toward the twenty-first century, you are building your career within a worldwide economic framework. The corporate clock now ticks to a global beat. What's more, the clock ticks at a faster rate than ever before in history. In order to achieve success within this new corporate culture, you will need to construct bold and innovative career paths to the future. Be assured it is possible. You can live exuberantly as a time-integrated person without endangering any of the success you rightly cherish.

The Old Future: Up the Ladder to Gold-Watch Time

As we look back on it now, the American corporation of the 1950s and 1960s seems like a dream. As an employee you were wrapped in a warm security blanket and taken care of as long as you obeyed the corporate guidelines. You could set up a time line that would take you to retirement and the gold watch as a reward for faithful service. You weren't promised the presidency of the company, necessarily, but you could count on being rewarded for hard work. Even mediocre or indifferent work would be tolerated if you were loyal. Your career ladder was placed before you, and if you didn't manage to climb all the way to the top, you could at least perch securely on whatever rung you reached. Some companies could be brutal back then, too, but there was a difference. The economy was booming. So many companies were expanding that, if a person got fired by one corporation, there were plenty of others around that were taking on management trainees by the truckload. By and large, the kind of corporation that offered employees a long-term future lasted through the 1970s. But over the last decade the extended time lines got pulled up. They exist only in memory now.

The Transformed Corporation: Time Is the New Prize

A new and highly sophisticated version of the old Ben Franklin maxim, "Time is money," is being applied throughout the American corporate culture today. In *Competing Against Time* (The Free Press, 1990), a recent book describing the ways in which time-based competition operates in our global economy, author George Stalk, Jr., points out, "Time consumption like cost is quantifiable and therefore manageable." He calls time the "fourth dimension of competitiveness," and maintains that, as a strategic weapon "time is the equivalent of money, productivity, quality, even innovation."

It's a new game, with new rules, and to be a winner you need to learn how to play. You need to understand the corporate clock which is now in operation. The question which the corporation asks about you is: how much is your time worth—on a minute-to-minute basis. But the question you need to ask is: how are you going to invest your time? Also, what returns do you expect when you join an organization that runs on fast time and offers you only a short-term guarantee? The new career paradigm you need to construct is above all a time paradigm, because the drastic changes in American corporate culture are time changes.

Most corporations run on a short time line at a constantly accelerating pace. What that means for millions of employees is daily pressure to work longer hours at a faster speed. The major themes of the 1990s— technological improvement, especially in telecommunications and computerization, compressed-time product cycles, and global competition—translate, for employees, into a work environment where time is the single most highly regarded standard of measurement.

Understanding the corporate culture and how you are placed within it is the essential first step to taking back ownership of your work time.

The New Future: No Ladder and No Gold Watch

Especially since 1980, American corporations have dramatically short-ened the time lines according to which goals are set, work is done, and profits are measured. They have switched from long-term to short-term planning. They've turned the clock from macro-time to micro-time. The future extends only to the end of the next quarter, with its entire contents contained in the bottom line. If short-term profitability means every-thing and long-range survival doesn't count, the consequence is a speeded-up work pace throughout the corporate culture, both inside individual companies and in the larger business environment, which now takes in the global economy.

Merger Mania: Getting Rich Quick

In this fast-time climate, top managers and chief executives have also sought short paths to riches for their corporations and themselves. As Lester Thurow points out in *The Zero-Sum Solution* (Simon & Schuster, 1986), "Instead of engaging in the lengthy process of growing and fine-tuning new products or processes at home, top managers came to feel they can get rich quick and expand their company with a well-timed takeover." Volcanic changes erupted. The quick fix based on the vision of huge and instantaneous profits became the new way of corporate think-ing in America. Mergers and acquisitions held a powerful, almost addic-tive appeal for American executives and their like-minded partners from around the world.

Between 1980 and 1989, W.T. Grimm & Co., which acts as a broker for buying and selling companies, tracked over 25,000 mergers or acquisi-tions. The stakes got gigantic. In 1984, the biggest merger in history oc-curred when Chevron acquired Gulf for over $13 billion. By 1989, the price leaped to $25 billion when Kohlberg, Kravis, Roberts & Company led a leveraged buyout of R.J.R. Nabisco, Inc.

At the same time, the gap between winners and losers widened. Typical employee fallout was large—the combined Gulf/Chevron work force, for example, was reduced from 79,000 to 61,000. R.J.R. Nabisco, Inc., dismissed 1,640 employees, or about 12 percent of the work force at its tobacco company. As the wild west mentality took hold, a new glamour vocabulary emerged to create an image of dynamic growth and positive reorganization of corporations, which masked the reality of what was happening to millions of displaced employees. Rhetoric and reality parted company. Images of suitors, white knights, raiders seeking "greenmail" (a new term for blackmail) to go away, and companies taking poison pills to save themselves obscured the fact that a few big winners gained at the expense of many losers. Managers were let go by the thousands across America.

The invention of junk bonds—high-risk paper put out at very high interest rates—speeded up the pace of mergers and acquisitions to an unimaginable degree. Suddenly every company was up for sale, whether it wanted to be or not. Some companies, trying to protect themselves from takeover, bailed out by letting employees go in large numbers. Others sold parts of their corporation as a survival technique. However, as Amanda Bennett notes in *The Death of the Organization Man,* "Much of the merger and acquisition business in the 1980s came from companies restructuring themselves of their own accord, spinning off some units that didn't fit their business, adding new ones that they thought did. For example, between 1981 and 1987, General Electric spent $11.1 billion to buy 338 businesses. During that same period, it sold 232 businesses worth $5.9 billion, and closed 73 plants and offices."

Getting Lean and Mean

To get lean and mean, as an expression, conjures up the Old West and the cowboys who did what it took to make a life in the wild open spaces stretching to the Pacific. But in the corporate culture of the eighties, it meant cutting as many employees from the payroll as was needed to get the bottom line at a profit level that satisfied shareholders. "The shareholder syndrome," Donald Frey, former Bell & Howell Company chairman, called the drive to satisfy shareholders by squeezing the last dollar of profitability out of a company. By the mid-eighties most companies had gotten hyper-aware of foreign competition and were running scared. The quick-fix formula for a company with a shaky bottom line was cutting costs by cutting personnel.

Although the giant corporations still paid lip service to the paternalism that reigned from the fifties through the seventies, it was at best a stern and punishing father at the helm. White-collar workers were dumped by the thousands, and those left in the offices had to pick up the slack. Insecurity crept quietly into the skyscrapers of America. Managers of the eighties felt the same fear that autoworkers and steelworkers had faced in the previous decades.

The Nineties: Short and Fragile Time Lines

The speed-up of corporate life, which makes so many workers frantic with the hurrying pace, shows no sign of abating. Quite the reverse.

There is an uncounted legion of managers in the early 1990s who have already been forced to hop from two or three organizations that got mean and lean at their expense. Inside companies, there is a thinner atmosphere: fewer promotions, fewer salary hikes, scaled-down benefits and pension packages. What's more, as Amanda Bennett puts it, "from now on, corporations won't be shy about letting go the people whom they no longer need." The emerging system is one "that is much more likely to perceive, and to treat, managers as costs, not assets."

As corporate restructuring continues, as companies no longer offer life-time security and the traditional career ladder for their employees, individual employees must find ways to flourish in an atmosphere where there is turbulence aplenty, but no easy answers. One investment banker told me, "The big challenge of the nineties will be to fix all these overleveraged companies." What she meant is that the mania to "do deals"—leveraged buyouts, multibillion-dollar mergers, and the amassing of huge empires—has resulted in staggering debt loads for hundreds of companies. Who is going to pay? The band-aid of downsizing, which is the glamour word for firing people, will continue to be applied. Employee layoffs will keep the bloodbath flowing.

Wayne's Time at Sears Mirrors Our Corporate Culture

Shortly after Wayne survived the Sears purge of 1989, as many employees referred to it, he said, "Sears tells us that we've downsized as much as we're going to—that we're at fighting weight now. But everybody at the office lays bets on when the next cuts will come." A few months after Wayne made this statement to me, the CEO of Sears took over personal direction of the financially weak Merchandise Group. The rumor was that he was under the gun from the board of directors to turn a profit within six months or be booted out himself; some 5,000 more layoffs were expected.

Wayne's anxiety is no less because he shares it with millions of other managers and professionals. Ironically, some managers who survived the tumult of earlier corporate reorganizations are worse off today than those who got fired—many of whom have parlayed sizable severance packages into new entrepreneurial careers.

In 1988, Wayne's initial reactions to the prospect of layoffs were similar to those of hundreds of thousands of others: panic, disbelief, emotional paralysis, anger, and depression. When he survived that first cut, he felt relieved at first and tried hard to believe in the company rhetoric that no more firings were contemplated.

Now Wayne realizes that a new corporate culture is in place not only at Sears but at corporations throughout the country. His task for the present is to move beyond his old feelings and learn how to become a winner in this new economic environment.

How Should You Invest Your Time?

You want to invest your time in order to assure yourself of success. The last thing you should do is waste time trying to live in the past; the dream world of the 1960s-style corporation no longer exists. Nor do you want to waste emotional energy—which also takes up valuable time that you need for other purposes—trying to avoid facing your own feelings about your worklife. Time pressures are here to stay. Futurists assure us that the marketplace of the 1990s and beyond will continue to be global in scope and ferociously competitive in spirit. Many American corporations have already adopted a posture of continuous restructuring. Key words are "fluid" and "process management." The glamour vocabulary describes this corporate culture in terms favorable to owners. But you must understand this world in terms useful to yourself. For employees, downsizing and delayering mean the loss of jobs or the fear of being displaced.

Looking for advice, I approached experts in management, executives in human resources from Fortune 500 companies, career officers at top universities, and people who have achieved success without being time-driven. I found one theme underlying all their counsel: *Face the new givens.* Operate realistically within the emergent global marketplace. You belong to the corporate culture of the 1990s. You can't change it, but you can learn to function in it with great effectiveness.

New Given #1: No Job Is Forever

A changed ambience prevails inside the corporations of America today. There is no longer a sense of security and stability, a confidence that your job will be there for you over the next decade or several decades. While a natural desire would lead you to say, "My job is different, my company is different," it is a risky conclusion. The cataclysmic worldwide economic and political events of the last few years have demonstrated that the only stable principle to be counted on is change itself. No job is forever, and good performance is not the protection it once was.

New Given #2: Employees Are Cost Units

In most organizations, people feel time pressures, if not every day, then on a seasonal basis. But the pressure to perform for longer hours at a faster pace has an additional underlying pressure. People are valued, in the time-based corporation, chiefly for their performance as measured in time segments which can be related to the balance sheet and annual report to stockholders. Head count, not employees, is the corporate way of thinking.

Employees, going all the way up to top management, are typically viewed as costs rather than assets on the balance sheet. Applied to you as an individual, the principle is this: Owners want to know exactly how much your time is worth to them, broken down into the smallest possible units of time. That unit will then be converted to the minimum salary and benefits that the market will bear.

The financial goal is to maximize profits while minimizing costs. Personnel costs figure largely in the computation, which is then related to the unit value of a share for stock. For example, General Motors decided to cut costs by $5 billion annually by closing 11 auto plants and by cutting 25 percent of its salaried employees. This cutback was translated into a saving of $8 per share of stock by the end of the decade.

Computers likewise play a role in the corporate zeal to cut personnel as a money-saving device. Shoshana Zuboff points out how management usually views computerization of a plant or office: "To justify a computer, we have to show job eliminations." In this way, the speed-up of work which the computer brings gets linked to the speed-up of employee terminations. While reducing head count within a department brings rewards to managers, the computer is also hastening the departure of the managers themselves.

New Given #3: The Covenant Is Broken

The covenant between owners and workers that exists in a corporation is ultimately based not on a piece of legal paper or on the company brochures that list terms and benefits, but upon mutual trust. The employment covenant exists as a promise and fundamental agreement of trust between two parties. Americans, in a long struggle that began with urbanization, industrialization, and the labor union movement, finally achieved—in the fifties, sixties, and seventies—a kind of ideal covenant, an understood promise of long-term employment in exchange for decent work and loyalty.

All that has changed. With the dramatic reorganization of corporate culture in the eighties, the covenant has been broken. After a takeover, or even amidst rumors that there will be one, employees are forced to do their work on a day-to-day basis, uncertain how much of a future lies before them. Mutual trust has disappeared with the demise of the long-term contract.

What Should You Do? Here's What Not to Do

When employees fear mergers, cutbacks, restructuring, downsizing, or delayering, their first response is to do exactly the worst thing in the world: put in even longer hours on the job, hoping thereby to buy job security for themselves. The new time-based corporate culture is one of instability and insecurity from the point of view of employees. Here is a list of things not to do as you are learning to take back ownership of your work time.

1. Don't work longer hours than you already do.
2. Don't start working harder on the job than you already do.
3. Don't tell yourself nothing has changed in your company.
4. Don't tell yourself that your own job is safe even if nobody else's is.
5. Don't waste time at the company rumor mill.
6. Don't step up efforts to win over your boss—he or she probably doesn't have the power of bygone days.
7. Don't waste time reading tea leaves on the job. The future isn't in them.
8. Don't feel that you're a victim.
9. Don't believe that you must accept an unfairly heavy workload.
10. Don't wear your heart on your shirtsleeves.

In avoiding these 10 negative steps, you will already have taken substantial action to reclaim ownership of your work time. You are eliminating unhealthy emotional reactions and paving the way for more positive action to build your future career.

Gaining a Foothold in a Slippery Environment

The smart employee headed for success in the nineties will be the time-integrated person, not the time-driven individual, because time urgency, especially when it becomes chronic and severe, destroys self-esteem, creativity, and concentration. These very skills are most prized in a corporate culture that lacks stability and security.

In accepting the givens of the corporate culture as it exists today, your most intelligent response is to change your worklife accordingly, not by dancing faster to somebody else's tune, but by becoming more firmly centered in yourself. You need to start by constructing a time-based action plan for yourself—a method for dealing successfully with the present—then move forward to construct a new career paradigm for the future.

Time management techniques may seem like the obvious solution, but they offer at best a short-term solution. Getting better organized down to the minute so as to manage an ever-heavier workload doesn't meet your long-term goals. Some time pressures are directly due to taking on the jobs of co-workers who lost their jobs in cutbacks; that could become a bottomless pit. You will be learning to manage your time and your career across companies, so it would be counterproductive to sink deeper into a time morass at your present company.

In order to build a solid, action-based plan for your future, you need to separate your own identity and career goals from those of your present company. A job is not a career. Since companies are not offering guarantees of long-term employment, it doesn't make sense to identify your future career plan with a single company. The career ladder paradigm is outmoded; you will be seeking a paradigm which will be workable in the global marketplace of the future. So instead of trying desperately to cling to old models that are gone, look for ways to flourish in the new environment. In the absence of mentors and "father figures" in the corporations, today's careerists need a new business community. This is what you will learn how to build.

What about Loyalty? A Realistic View

Life doesn't begin and end at the front door of your present company. The model of employee loyalty should change to go along with the altered structure of the corporate culture today. You owe loyalty primarily to yourself—not in an egocentric, selfish way, but in a realistic way which recognizes that the company is not a father willing and able to take care of you, so long as you're good, for the rest of your working life. The simple fact is that you're "safe" only as long as your combination of skills meets the needs of the company you're with, which is in an ever-fluid situation.

Whenever you have a choice, try to do things that are good for you as well as for the company. Understand that I'm not suggesting you shortchange your employer or in any way perform less than competently. What I'm saying is that you should measure your efforts for the company against the standard of the rewards which the company offers you. The principle you want to operate with is fairness on both sides rather than mindless subservience on your part.

Evaluate Your Present Company

No company is forever, and no corporation is perfect, but there are better and worse organizations. In the past, a young college graduate would look

at the starting salary, advancement potential, vacation policy, and benefits package, and maybe take a glance at "working conditions"—or the
corporate ambience. Now, when long-term job security is not a realistic
expectation, it makes sense to take a look at your present workplace,
whether you've been there one year or fifteen, with the question of how
rewarding and enjoyable your time is.

Of the many corporations where I've spent time giving communications seminars to managers, professionals, and executives, the very best
time-integrated environment was the Johns Hopkins University Applied Physics Lab in Laurel, Maryland. Before my first trip there, I
expected that the time ambience would be super-pressured, because the
research done there includes top-secret design and testing of our national defense arsenal. But quite to the contrary, it was one of the most
pleasant, exhilarating, and stimulating workplaces I've encountered.
Employees from top scientists to secretaries seemed happy, committed,
purposeful, yet completely unharried. It was an organization at which
some of the best creative work in the country gets done, yet nobody
seemed hurried.

At the other extreme was a bank in the Mid-Atlantic region which I
won't name, where the atmosphere reminded me of a speeded-up Charlie
Chaplin movie. Everybody rushed around so much, with an air of such
extreme time urgency, that it was impossible to concentrate. The group of
senior vice presidents whom I taught were so distracted and restless that
they had developed very short attention spans. I couldn't wait to get out of
there.

Where on the spectrum does your company fit in? Take a minute to fill
in the corporate quiz below.

Corporate Quiz
Is Your Company Time-Integrated?

	YES	NO
1. Does your company expect you to work more than 40 hours weekly as a matter of course?	____	____
2. Does your boss often call you at home?	____	____
3. Is your office a rumor mill about takeovers, cutbacks, weak profits, and the like?	____	____
4. Is your workload too heavy?	____	____

5. Do you feel pressured to work at a pace that goes past your comfort zone?   ____ ____

6. Does your boss set unrealistic deadlines?   ____ ____

7. Is the office time ambience harried?   ____ ____

8. Does your boss monitor your time excessively?   ____ ____

9. Does your company regard shareholders as more important than employees?   ____ ____

10. Does your company refuse to share its future plans with you and other employees?   ____ ____

TOTALS   ____ ____

Scoring Key. Count the number of "yes" answers.

0 to 4   Your company's time expectations are average.

5 to 7   The atmosphere is time-pressured, but there may be room for negotiating improvements.

8 to 10   The time pressures are severe. You may want to consider other companies.

Questions to Ponder

Your new career paradigm will arise not only out of the skills you are learning, but also out of the insights you will gain by becoming aware of your time on the job in a fresh way—not as clock service monitored by others, but as the time of your life being spent in furtherance of your own goals of self-realization. Consider the questions below as issues to turn over in your mind in a leisurely fashion. Surprising solutions may greet you when least expected. These will not be magical answers, but rather the fruit of your creative imagination at play. What you are teaching yourself is an innovative method for solving problems.

- How can I succeed without turning all my time over to my career?
- What dangers should I be wary of?
- What strategies do I need?
- What can I learn from time-integrated people?
- What should I do about my present job?

Early Steps Toward a New Career Paradigm

1. Recognize that the task of constructing a new career paradigm for yourself will be hard work and not easily accomplished, but nonetheless it is a worthwhile, indeed essential, effort.
2. Believe in yourself. Don't give anybody else the power over your time. Play your own game, not somebody else's.
3. Understand power. The only kind of power worth going after is power over your own time. Can you direct your own destiny, or are you time's plaything?

11

TURNING TIME PRESSURE AT WORK TO YOUR ADVANTAGE

Who gains time gains everything.

—DISRAELI, *TANCREDI*

There is an old Seneca Indian saying which goes: "The earth is full of supernatural helpers who aid those of a good mind." In this chapter you will learn how to be a successful time-integrated achiever in a time-pressured corporate culture. I will give you strategies for advancing your career while getting your job done. I want to show you how to take back time for yourself *on the job*, and then how to use this newly reclaimed time to best advantage for yourself. The key, of course, is learning how to do this without jeopardizing your position or turning yourself into a cynic or a fraudulent employee. As you will see, the wonderful irony is that the better you truly serve your own best ends, the better your work performance will be.

Time is what matters most in life. Perhaps up till now you thought of time on the job as "company time," and therefore largely out of your control. This is defeatist thinking. You can have mastery of all your time if you decide to take the reins yourself. If you have needlessly handed over too much of your time to your employer, you have to figure out how to "buy" it back. This is a serious strategic issue. First of all, you are operating in a corporate environment where 60-hour weeks seem normal. Second, your employer has gotten used to the profligate use of your time and won't want to give it up without a struggle.

Time is the new negotiable, and you need to become a shrewd negotiator. There are two ways to "buy back" work time: 1) You can actually spend less time at the office by cutting back your hours substantially; or 2) you can transform the way you spend your time on the job. The second alternative is the most promising. If you were suddenly to stage a major retreat from the office, you would make yourself very visible by your absence and thus very vulnerable.

Work in Micro-Time, Think in Macro-Time

In New York, The Wyatt Company offers seminars to teach top American executives how to serve corporate goals through time-based competition—which they call "one of the newest competitive weapons to appear in the global market." One of these courses is taught by Dr. Eiji Mizutani, director of Wyatt's Tokyo office. Based on the truism, "time is money," the course describes two contrasting views of time. Says Mizutani, "In the U.S. business community, time is viewed as something controllable, and something to be saved as much as possible. Time tends to be addressed only as *micro-time.* As such, the view fosters a short-term perspective. In contrast, in Europe and Japan, time is something given, and should be used to the fullest. Time may be said to be treated as *macro-time.* As it is, this view leads to a long-term perspective.

"The two views of time are by nature not contradictory to each other but are complementary to one another," he continues. "On the tactical level, the short-term perspective and micro-time are necessary, but without the long-term perspective and macro-time, they are not sufficient to come up to the strategic level and complete the picture."

This is a useful distinction which you can easily apply to your work time. In your day-to-day, hour-by-hour efforts on the job, work in micro-time. Do what needs to be done efficiently to meet your company's expectations. At the same time, think in macro-time. Free yourself mentally from the constraints of the corporate clock to spend your time in accordance with your long-term career goals. After all, if micro-time and macro-time can be blended successfully to attain corporate goals, the same strategy will be effective for you as an individual.

What Is Your Macro-Time Goal?

Futurist writers today make a distinction between a "high standard of living" and a "high quality of life." The first expression, which used to be popular in the decades of the seventies and eighties, refers mainly to material possessions: cars, houses, vacation chalets, furs, jewels, and so on—all the things money can buy. But the new phrase for the nineties, "high quality of life," refers to the pleasures of a specifically human life: family, friends, laughter and relaxation, personal achievements and satisfactions, and the leisure to pursue the interests that enrich us as people. One of the most essential measures of this kind of life is the amount of time available to spend with other people in pursuit of what matters most to us.

Thus we see time—not harried, driven, distracted time, but rich, full, integrated time—as the greatest prize to be sought, more important than money and all the things it can buy. Your time is your life. It doesn't stop being less a prize or less your own when you step inside your company's doors. You want to get rid of time urgency on the job just as much as in your personal life. If you take hold of this basic thought, you will naturally begin to view your time on the job through a clearer lens.

Take Charge of Your Time: Be Bold and Innovative

Robert Galvin, the phenomenally successful CEO of Motorola Inc., said recently in *Business Month* that in this era of tough global competition, it is necessary for corporations to have a long-term strategic vision which they have the boldness to implement on a grand scale. "The best players of the game will be better anticipators of change, willing to commit resources freely and determined to stay the course," he said.

Just as the majority of corporations are restructuring and, in the process, developing new ideas, strategies, and skills for successfully meeting the challenge of global competition, so must you. From the corporation's point of view as a time-based global competitor, you as an individual have value only insofar as your skills meet its constantly fluctuating needs. But you are learning to manage your career, as well as your life taken as a whole, not according to the corporate clock, but according to your own large vision—boldly conceived and courageously implemented. Keep this picture of yourself in your mind as you start each workday. Your time belongs to you.

Cast Your Time Lines Beyond Your Company's Door

Whether you plan to stay at your present job, because you love it, or whether you plan to leave doesn't really make any difference right now. Given the instability and insecurity of the corporate culture, you still need to transform your time on the job. So at the very least, you want to bring another kind of time—your own time, the time that respects your circadian rhythms, your own internal sense of the right pace for you, as it ebbs and flows throughout the day—to your work time.

While you must be aware of the ticking of the company clock on micro-time, you want to manage your days according to macro-time, your long-range career goals. Rather than identifying your career with your company's clock, start throwing time lines beyond your company's front door. Whatever choices are yours to make on the job should be made with the longer time lines in mind. You can integrate all these various time lines on the job.

No Job Is Finished until You Get Credit for It

Let's face it: there are people who work full-time to take credit for other people's work. Any company you walk into is full of stories about how a given employee got credit for somebody else's work.

I've observed that people who are true performers tend to operate in just the opposite way—to care so much for doing a good job that they neglect to have it recognized. In these times you can't afford to bury your light under a bushel. Remember that it's not enough to be competent; you must be *perceived* as competent by your superiors and by those in your community of business friends who support your professional goals. Your value to your company serves your purposes only if those in command are knowledgeable about your ongoing achievements. This takes a lot of energy, which is why the self-nurturing program I presented to you in Part II should not be neglected, no matter how busy you are.

I'm not suggesting that you convert yourself into an unbearable egoist. That would be counterproductive. Rather you need simply to realize that a project is not completely finished until you have communicated your accomplishment to your superiors. This is a realistic strategy for maintaining your viability in your present company while getting into the habit of acting assertively according to your own time lines.

Don't Just Hang On while Your Job Disappears

Learn new skills. Futurists Marvin Cetron and Owen Davies, in their recent book, *American Renaissance* (St. Martin's Press, 1989) write, "Most of the new jobs that appear, not just in the 1990s but from now on, will fall into only two categories: the ones you don't want and the ones you can't get—not, at least, without extensive preparation." They explain, "As firms become information-based, they stop hiring people with generalized management skills and sign on specialists to work in task-focused teams." These teams are usually organized as independent entities which report directly to top management. In this kind of corporate environment, the more you know and the more different kinds of information you can deal with, the more valuable you are—both within your present company and at other organizations.

Enhance Your Employability: Have Skills, Will Travel

Go all out for learning. Upgrade, expand, and develop your skills. Resist the pressure to become ever more narrowly specialized. A top executive of a multinational firm told me that the average newcomer will spend about three years with his firm. "During that time," he said, "the only way I can mentor that person is to help put a few more arrows in the quiver." Skills are arrows of the most necessary kind. Whenever you have a choice, undertake company projects which will enhance or develop your skills rather than merely use already well-established knowledge and expertise. Are there "white spaces" in your department that you could fill with a useful project from which you could learn something valuable to you?

What does the company offer in projects which will enhance your *résumé*, add to your knowledge, broaden your range of experiences, allow your creativity to be expressed, give you opportunities for meeting and communicating with others in your field? These are the macro-time standards you seek to apply every day.

Think of formal training and education. The first place to look for potential new training is your own company. What training does it offer you? What seminars and courses will it pay for you to take elsewhere, particularly on company time? What education will it either pay for, or give you time off to get?

Investigate education and training options in your local community—both short-term and long-term. As you think about enhancing your employability today, you will naturally tend to think about next year and the years beyond. Thinking smart in micro-time leads you to macro-time planning.

Perhaps you can flip an apparent negative into a positive. Some companies have slowed down their promotion track considerably, but will encourage employees to move laterally to other departments. Would another department provide the challenge of new skills and information which would enhance your employability? If so, the prospect may be worth pursuing.

Let your creative imagination take flight on the subject of new skills. Don't be afraid to stray far afield—into foreign languages or history or mathematics or third-world economics. Looking for tie-ins beyond the most obvious kinds of refresher courses may give you unexpected new ideas.

Some years back, when I was an academic dean at Loyola Evening College in Baltimore, a woman sat down to discuss her future. She had gotten her bachelor's degree in business and had a good job, but felt she wouldn't advance without getting a graduate business degree, the MBA.

"I would like to do that, but I figure, going part-time at night, it will take me five years, and I'll be 38 by then," she said apprehensively.

"And how old will you be in five years," I asked her, "if you don't go into the master's program?"

Adopt a Careful Financial Lifestyle

In uncertain times, be sensible and live below your means. I interviewed an investment banker who specialized in junk-bond merger deals throughout the 1980s, and whose income topped $2 million annually. "My husband and I deal exclusively in cash," she told me. "We have no debts, no mortgage, no credit card balances." You might say, well, if I had that income, neither would I. But the truth is that Wall Street is lined with top-flight professionals who got left out in the cold and have debts which add enormously to their pressure. They had adopted a financial lifestyle which consumed all their income.

Even if you're a top performer with high income, you can't be sure of long-term job security.

Micro-Time Fixes: Improving Things Right Now

The worst time trap you can fall into is to say to yourself, "I'm too busy to figure out how to get the time pressure out of my work." Even if you've concluded that your present company falls short and you need to look elsewhere, you can still improve your situation. No matter how harried the environment, you can take charge of your work time. Scan the micro-time environment, and analyze it for your purposes. Before you can focus creatively on your future, you need to improve things in the immediate present. You need to invent "thinking space" for yourself. No work task merits greater attention than this.

Eight Useful Ways to Spend Dead Time at Work

In most organizations, there's plenty of dead time. Some of the most whipped-up companies contain pockets of wasted time—you're waiting for a phone call to come through, a meeting to start, or a caller to arrive. Or you're stuck at a boring meeting that lasts forever and contains nothing of value to your job. Look around and you'll probably see a pattern of "white spaces" that you could regard as stretches of empty time for yourself—thinking time. Don't feel guilty. Don't justify. Just tune into your own personal agenda and think about it. This is using micro-time for macro-time projects—your future. Of course, to be useful, these thinking times must have an agenda worked out during periods when you have significant creative time to develop one.

Once, I was scheduled to give an out-of-town seminar and arrived only to find out that an emergency corporate meeting required the last-minute postponement of my seminar for three hours—too short a period for me to leave that company and attend to other business. For the interim I was offered coffee, desk space, and paper. After a few minutes of distress (I had no other materials with me except what I needed for that presentation), I set to work on a difficult article that needed an overall structure. Up till then I'd been writing it in bits and pieces. The sudden appearance of a stretch of time plus a blank sheet of paper enabled me to conceptualize the article and get it outlined. After that session I was easily able to finish the work in odd bits of time.

When you find yourself with a "white space" of time, pay attention to your circadian rhythms. Are you high-energy or low-energy when the time presents itself? How much time lies before you? Would you rather be with people or alone? Make decisions spontaneously based on these feelings: they're the most "you" at the moment. Here are some suggestions:

- Work on updating your résumé.
- Go through stacks of paper in a "tossing-out" mood.
- Vegetate. No kidding. Air out your brain a little while.
- Get acquainted with new people at your workplace.
- Call a business friend and schedule a lunch.
- Call a business friend just to touch base.
- Read an article in a worthwhile journal.
- Take a walk.

Buy Back The Personal Time You Gave Away

If you've gotten into the habit of spending many more hours a week on the job than you really want to or feel you should have to, then you need to work out a careful set of tactics for getting back some of that time. Above all, go slowly. You didn't fall into this rut overnight, so you can't expect to get out of it in a week. But you can downsize your work time so that it doesn't take up a monstrous chunk of your life. Start with modest goals:

1. "I will reclaim first one hour a week, then two hours a week." It doesn't matter how you reclaim them, whether in 15-minute segments or in a single evening leaving on the dot at 5 P.M. The important thing is that you decide never to give back those hours to the job. A major Japanese department store recently announced that it was shortening the work week by 10 minutes a day and giving employees a holiday on their birthday.

2. Look to see where the slack is. Say you're one of those lucky people who lives only 10 or 15 minutes away from your workplace. The trouble is, you've gotten into the bad habit of running into the office for a couple of hours on Saturday mornings. Take back your Saturdays even if this means working a bit later for a few Fridays until your workload adjusts to the fact of life that you forbid yourself to go to the office on weekends. Reason this way: The people who live an hour and a half away wouldn't dream of going in; why should you recast an advantage into a disadvantage?

3. Learn the art of saying "no" to overtime requests without making your boss mad. Demonstrate that it is in the company's interest for you not to get overprogrammed from too much workhorse activity. Use psychology! Negotiate time slots. Think of yourself as a winning racehorse, not a plodding nag. Communicate images of yourself as smart and savvy, not a drone who never lifts eyes from the desktop terminal.

4. Get out of the habit of stuffing your briefcase with work to bring home. Start making sharper distinctions between work time and personal time.

5. Discourage business calls to your home.

6. Make sure you use up all holiday and vacation time.

Pacing Yourself on the Job

Pacing yourself on the job means making an effort to do what you want to within the actual constraints, not the self-imposed restraints. I've noticed that people often say, "I can't do this," when there is actually no barrier at all.

Rushing too much and working on too-short time lines destroys the real pleasure of work. Begin to look at what you do on the job as capable of offering you satisfaction in the present moment. Look for enjoyment in what you are doing now. See it as an end in itself as well as something leading you another step upward.

Some problems need time to mature. Let your creative subconscious work on some of the tough nuts. The solution may "pop up" and surprise you. In overcoming time urgency on the job, you are adopting a work style which leaves time for things to develop "on their own" without always overcontrolling daily events. More time, money, and human resources have been spent on fixing a hurried project than if they had been done right the first time around.

Mayor Kurt Schmoke of Baltimore, a highly intelligent, Harvard-educated, 39-year-old, took an emergency trip to the hospital early in his mayoral term with what appeared to be a heart attack. He had the classic symptoms: chest pains, shortness of breath, and so on. The diagnosis, fortunately, was a spasm of the esophagus, which Mayor Schmoke said he didn't feel was brought on by stress but rather by "a rushed lifestyle that includes swallowing lunch on the run, drinking too much soda and failing to get enough exercise." The episode understandably gave the mayor a scare and brought him to a decision to alter this frantically paced lifestyle. He said, "This was just a good reminder that you can take care of a lot of things, but you also have to take care of yourself."

Smart Ways to Get Extended Project Deadlines

1. Remembering that time is the hottest new negotiable, begin to draw your own time lines at the workplace. You can prevent some (if not all) time pressures by anticipating them. Suggest due dates for projects which give you ample time. Present a rationale and a work schedule which emphasize quality results. Link flexible time lines and the need for creative time to successful results. Break the project into time segments that add up to a longer total time allowance than you would otherwise have gotten.

2. Circulate interim reports about ongoing projects. Suggest adjusted deadlines as soon as you suspect difficulties in completing the project on deadline. Don't wait till the deadline arrives.

3. Introduce your boss to the concept of short-term overtime, which is tied not to habit but to specific projects. Get your supervisors gradually educated to the idea that overtime should be unusual.

4. Buy creative time for yourself. Ted Cassera, a successful owner of a New Jersey engineering firm, shared one of his tactics with me. His firm had just taken on a tremendous plum of a project—a large development of luxury custom homes with an Arnold Palmer Championship golf course as its centerpiece—expected to be one of the best in the country. The problem was that the mayor of the town put Ted's firm on too short a time line. He wanted the development fully designed and ready for construction within six months so that he could start taxing the owners and filling up the town coffers. Ted realized his firm couldn't do top-notch design and planning, even putting all the firm's resources into

the project, within that short a time frame. It was a delicate issue. If he questioned the deadline publicly, he would lose face—and maybe the project. So he privately approached the Japanese partner.

"Look," said Ted, "we can crank out the building plans in six months if that's what you want. No problem. But if you want something really spectacular for this Arnold Palmer Championship golf course, well then, we're going to need some additional time to do it right."

Ted sat back and waited. He had observed that the American partner was overly eager to please the mayor. "If the mayor said jump, this guy asked, 'How high?'" The Japanese partner, on the other hand, had no particular interest in pleasing the mayor by finishing the project quickly. As Ted had expected, the American and Japanese partners hammered out a new deadline, and within a few days, the engineering firm had the additional time needed to do a first-rate job.

5. Think through the time requirements of a project before you take it on. If you love your work, as I do, you tend to jump into an exciting project without carefully thinking through the time requirements. Budget and finances, yes; but time, no. Secure sufficient resources to do a project well. One highly successful corporate executive I interviewed had recently helped negotiate a huge corporate merger, then got the task of reorganizing the stock portfolios of the new management team. He accepted the high-priority project enthusiastically, but took care at the outset to build ample resources into his planning. He assembled a competent staff, realizing that big jobs done under a short time line require extra resources. A trusted assistant who supervised the data gathering hired two temporary clerks.

Then this executive focused on himself, scheduling a getaway weekend three months down the line: his reward and incentive to keep his creative energy high during the project. In addition, he has planned refueling time midway through the project—a Sunday dinner at a favorite country inn, a leisurely lunch with a friend who has nothing to do with this project. This executive doesn't waste his talent: he nourishes it.

6. Plan time rewards for yourself at the conclusion of projects that demand long hours. Trust yourself enough to admit that, although you're a wonderfully energetic person, you're not superhuman, nor do you aspire to be. Analyze your limitations and acknowledge them to your supervisors—at the beginning of a project, when a few days' rest can be programmed into the plan.

7. Establish project-driven time lines. I interviewed numerous researchers at the Johns Hopkins University Applied Physics Lab, where important defense work is conducted. One scientist said that the flexible deadlines are among the most enjoyable aspects of his job. "There is very little 'heat' from management," he told me. "Most deadlines are few

and far between." What goes along with the relaxed time lines, said another researcher, are "creative fulfillment, low stress, and a friendly atmosphere among colleagues." A project engineer reported that the best part of his job is "being able to define, at least to some extent, what I have to do." Autonomy gives these people the time to go with the natural rhythm of problem solving. One would expect here, if anywhere, a high-stress environment, but the word they all use instead is: challenge. They enjoy a learning environment where friendship with colleagues springs up naturally.

8. Remember that this is an era when every company believes it must have a super-fast product cycle from design phase to marketing. Fight that! Argue for the long-range profit potential of quality products.

Good Signs

Becoming a time-integrated person doesn't happen overnight. But as you begin to put these new procedures, behaviors, attitudes, and strategies into effect, you'll begin to notice small victories, good signs that freedom lies ahead. You may notice that you're enjoying some of the small things in life that you had gotten out of the habit of noticing, that you laugh more easily, glance at your watch or the clock less frequently, go over lists in your mind less obsessively, occasionally feel less tired at the end of the day, have more energy when the day starts some mornings. You may also discover that you're less concerned with your present company's future as you begin to focus on your own years ahead. Good! This means you're on your way.

Quick Fix Quiz: How Are You Doing?

Before you go any further, take stock. Is your time on the job beginning to serve your purposes? Can you answer *yes* to all the questions below?

1. Are your career skills portable?

2. Are you working at employability enhancement?

3. Do you maintain high visibility?

4. Do you stay as fluid as your company?

5. Are you learning portable new skills on the job?

6. Are you getting proper recognition?

7. Have you recently updated your résumé?

8. Are you alert to opportunities in your field?

9. Do you take advantage of company-paid training?

Benefits: Getting Your Time's Worth

The greater your qualifications and skills, and the better you are at marketing yourself, the greater your power to negotiate time for yourself. Whether you're thinking of staying at your present company or planning a change, you still need to cast a critical eye on the company's benefits package. Cast your inquiries about benefits into a time orientation. When you're not being promised long-term employment, the retirement package drops to secondary status. The more relevant question becomes: Can I take accumulated retirement benefits, or any portion of them, with me when I leave this company—whether voluntarily or not?

While you will certainly examine and evaluate a company's pension program before you accept a job, you must be realistic, figuring that your chance of ever cashing in on that program—if you're in you're twenties, thirties, or forties, is pretty minimal. Will the company still be around? Will it keep you around? Will you still want to be around? How many times will the company change its pension program before you get ready to accept it?

The urgent question is: What is the company willing to do about the time pressures I live with *now?* Salary, job status, and advancement opportunities are only the beginning of the benefits issue. For many workers, time is equally important to money. Particularly for many single parents, time is of the essence to their needs.

In the company's benefits package, find out what it offers that you can cash in from Day One on the job. Especially, what kind of time-help is available? How many annual paid days off are you given for holidays, vacation, personal days, sick leave? That's for starters. In Italy, for example, the majority of workers spend 11 months of the year on the job and are paid for 13. Virtually the entire population goes on vacation for the month of August. In Germany, workers at the BMW plant have a 35-hour week.

You owe it to yourself to obtain the best time benefits possible.

Paid Parental Leave: Reasonable Time Off

If you have a child, or expect you may have one in the foreseeable future, then benefits available to parents are crucially important. Paid leave for both the mother and father is a reasonable expectation—many countries in Europe have offered such benefits for years. But certainly for the mother it should be given. A reasonable period of unpaid leave time for a new mother ought to be available as well. IBM Corporation grants new mothers leaves of up to three years with benefits and guarantees their jobs. But at this writing, relatively few American companies can boast of attractive parental leave programs. Among that minority are Colgate-Palmolive, Aetna Life & Casualty, and Merck & Co. in Rahway, New Jersey. You may be able to negotiate a clause in your employment contract if you're signing up with a company at a high enough level. In any event, *ask* for these benefits. As more and more highly qualified workers demand this, companies will eventually have to comply.

At one company where I served as consultant, I met two highly intelligent professionals who both worked for the company. When they had their first child, they worked out in advance a plan with the company, whereby the father went on a compressed time schedule and the mother went on a short-term, part-time schedule, with no loss in status for either of them.

Negotiating Time for Motherhood

Mary Herlihy, director of recruiting for the Johns Hopkins School of Nursing, spent many weeks in the latter part of her pregnancy planning how the departmental work could get done in the early weeks after the birth of her baby. She organized a detailed schedule, then presented it successfully to her boss well before her due date.

Nancy Evans, president and publisher of Doubleday, Inc., recently wrote: "When I was starting out in publishing, older women used to say to me, 'Well, you're never going to have a child, are you? That'll wreck your career.' I finally did choose to have a child—and I still have my career." She continued, "During the last few weeks of my pregnancy, we set up a fax machine at my house, brought in an assistant, and held meetings at my home. There are ways of doing this so that business doesn't stop and women don't get exhausted."

I say especially to my women readers, as somebody who has been there: Don't stay trapped in the supermom syndrome or the mommy track. They're both cheats. It's understandable if you've fallen in. But now focus on getting out; you don't belong there.

Day Care: Time Worth More Than Gold

An old Chinese proverb goes, "An inch of time cannot be bought for an inch of gold." Women like to have their small children nearby—within inches of them, if possible. If Stephanie, the mother and talented magazine editor you met in the first chapter, had the company benefit of on-site day care, or extra pay toward her private arrangements, it would have freed up her emotional energy and a good deal of her time. And millions of American women are in a similar position. The U.S. Labor Department estimates that 84 percent of all women of childbearing age will be working by 2000. Apple Computer, Inc. runs an in-house child-care center and gives $500 to each employee's new baby. Merck & Co. has donated land and money for a child-care facility and allows mothers to work at home. They are among the Top 10 of the 60 American companies considered best for working mothers by *Working Mother* magazine. The force of numbers will eventually dictate that day-care benefits become commonplace; you may as well start asking now.

Elder Care: Time for Helping Your Parents

According to population experts, the need to provide for elderly parents will soon affect a much larger group of American employees, from chief executives to secretaries. Almost one-third of all working adults are responsible for providing some care for an elderly person. Some have called the post-World War II baby boomers the "grieving generation" because so many of their parents are living into an old age of dependency. Some 300 companies in this country have already started programs to help employees take care of their older loved ones. Ask if elderly parents can be included in your health insurance benefits.

Wellness Programs

If a company offers a well-equipped fitness center, plus trained health information personnel, plus exercise instructors, that is a very strong benefit. You save both the time and money of going to a health club or other exercise center. You have the incentive to work out right where you work, which is good for your health, and you get the extra benefit of camaraderie with your colleagues. If a company is enlightened enough to offer such facilities on its own time, that's great. But it is a time benefit in any case because it saves you an extra bit of transportation. I remember vividly when I taught a course at Maryland National Bank in Newark, Delaware.

I visited their beautifully equipped, hi-tech fitness center. It contained the latest exercise equipment in a large mirrored room. The center opened every day at 6 A.M., and an instructor was available.

Flextime and Flexplace

The time is fast approaching when you will be able to work at home and choose your own hours, even as a salaried full-time employee of a corporation. This kind of flexibility not only enables you to save transportation time, but to pace yourself at exactly the style and rate you feel comfortable with—working according to your own rhythms. Flexible work schedules will become more commonplace during the 1990s, along with job sharing and work at home, according to a survey by the Conference Board, a business-supported research organization which surveyed 521 of the nation's biggest companies and found that 93 percent offer at least one kind of flexible staffing. The survey showed that the main beneficiaries of these programs as they now operate are women in clerical, administrative support, or sales positions. Managers, professionals, and executives generally do not have flexible schedules. But Kathleen Christensen, a City University of New York professor who compiled the study, said companies are coming under pressure to offer flexible staffing because of the tight labor market.

Futurists predict that by 2000, perhaps 20 percent of the American workforce will choose to work at home, communicating by computer, telephone, and fax machine with the office. Cetron and Davies, in *American Renaissance*, write, "Among information workers—roughly 44 percent of the labor force at the turn of the century—up to half will be able to work wherever they find it most convenient." When you have the freedom to allocate your time as you see fit, and also to create an environment that makes you happy to work in, this measurably expands your enjoyment of your time. (For a thorough exploration of this subject, read *Creating a Flexible Workplace: How to Select and Manage Alternative Work Options*, by Barney Olmsted and Suzanne Smith, Amacon, 1989.)

Tin Parchutes Are Future Protection

In today's short-term corporate culture, you are most valuable as an employee when you are being recruited to join the company. You have the greatest leverage for negotiation at this point. Golden parachutes—lucrative contracts providing multiple benefits to executives when they lose their jobs—are filtering down the corporate hierarchy. As they float downward, they change to tin, but are being widely demanded neverthe-less by job candidates at all levels. Tin parachutes are pre-employment severance agreements designed to protect lower-level executives and man-agers who stand in jeopardy of future job loss. In an era when takeover-induced staff cuts seem likely to go on indefinitely, it is eminently sensible to try to negotiate benefits applicable when the contract ends. Lynn Tendler Bignell, a partner in Gilbert-Tweed Associates, a recruiting com-pany, said in a recent *New York Times* article, "Today, nearly half our candi-dates get the agreements."

That number jumps up to nearly 80 percent if the job is in the con-sumer products arena, according to Sidney G. Stricker, a principal of Stricker, Sur & Associates, recruitment specialists in that field.

"We're having to give in to get good people," said a human resources vice president for an investment bank. A high-level executive for a cos-metics company no longer even tries to resist. "I've seen too many people left in the lurch when a company changes hands," he said. "If a candidate doesn't ask for an agreement, I'll suggest it myself."

The article reported that among the items in some recent agreements are: free use of the company's products for 5 years after termination—long-distance phone service from telephone companies, air travel from airlines, hotel accommodations from hotel chains; lifetime continuation of employee discounts on company products such as televisions and furniture; immediate vesting in a pension plan, with substantial payouts guaranteed; and continuation of medical benefits for as long as it takes to get another job.

When All Your Time Serves Your Purposes

Entrepreneurs starting up new businesses work longer hours than almost any other class of worker in America. The saving grace is that all your time belongs unquestionably to you. The pace you work at is entirely deter-mined by you, and all the rewards of success go directly to you. The time sacrifices you make are all for yourself, not a corporate owner or a stock-holder.

Worksteaders and telecommuters, independent contractors, and small entrepreneurs working from a home office are becoming an increasing proportion of the workforce. It is estimated that some 15 million people now list a home address as their principal place of business. Many women are leaving traditional jobs to build businesses they can operate at home as they raise children—a way of having their time for motherhood more fully.

Can you pick up the pieces after a corporate layoff? Is it possible to quit a dull or demeaning job, trading up to a more rewarding line of work? Yes. Even in mid-life. Self-employment is more than the great American dream. It is also a way to turn a dead end into an open road, achieving success limited only by your skills, persistence, and ingenuity.

If you decide to start your own business, experts advise that you not only assess carefully the skills you can bring to a business, but assemble a team to proceed along with you. In spite of the popular notion of the entrepreneur as a lone ranger, there is much to gain by joining forces with others. It's also easier to get financing if you have a team. According to management expert Tom Peters, every business should start off with a detailed business plan. This document serves as a framework for how the business will be run, how it will position itself in the marketplace and how it will get its message out to customers. The plan should also include a timetable for growth, projecting where the business should be in one year, two years, three years, and so on. Patience is necessary. No matter how much time you give the business to achieve its goals, chances are it will take longer.

Looking Toward the Future

The information and strategies in this chapter are geared to helping you transform the time of your present worklife. Taking back ownership of your time on the job frees you to enjoy your work more, putting out effort at a pace that feels right to you—slowing down and speeding up as your natural energy levels ebb and flow, allowing your creativity to grow and develop naturally. Your employer is not as important as the amount of freedom you have to work from within yourself and not as a slave to the clock.

Now, turning to the next chapter, you will learn how to construct a unique career paradigm for your future. What you need is a paradigm which takes into account the realities of the corporate culture as it races toward the twenty-first century, and which also answers your need for living your time to the fullest both within the workplace and outside it.

12

FIVE RINGS OF POWER: A NEW CAREER PARADIGM

All times are not alike.

—CERVANTES, *Don Quixote*

t was a sunny afternoon in May, and I was looking forward to a leisurely lunch with an old friend, a highly placed executive of a multinational company. We were meeting at a charming inn tucked away in a bucolic corner of a sprawling university campus. Richard called it his hideaway.

At first sight of him I saw how changed he was from our last lunch some eight months previously. Dark circles underlined his pale blue eyes which wore a worried expression, and his usually buoyant smile seemed tentative. Our conversation took a serious turn as we glanced over the menu.

The recurring theme in Richard's talk was this: In today's corporate world you can't anticipate anymore. How do you plan when you can't anticipate? "We used to routinely do strategic planning ten years ahead. Now nobody plans five years ahead. The strategic plan is for three years, and the current year is the operational year of the three-year plan, so it is really two years in advance." He shrugged. "It's no fun anymore."

In a meditative mood, Richard mulled over the way the new power structure works in this time-driven environment. "The pow wow council is the inside decision-making body. Trust is very important here. This circle has gotten tighter, more secretive. Whether the decisions are good or bad depends on the advisers and the quality of their data. Next comes the campfire. That is very close to the pow wow council, but not in it. Everybody wants to sit at the campfire, but most members of the organization realize they are somewhere between the outside periphery of the campfire and the inside edge of the wagon—there's a fairly big space in that area. Beyond the outside edge of the wagon, you're out of the picture." I couldn't help thinking: That's where the overwhelming number of employees in any organization find themselves.

Richard paused for a moment. Then he asked rhetorically, "Why does everybody carry a cellular phone everywhere he goes? Out of deep anxiety, insecurity—the fear that the powwow council will do something against him while his back is turned."

He regarded me broodingly. "What do you do in the face of constant change when it's impossible to anticipate?"

New times bring new problems, demanding new solutions. In uncertain times with no long-term employment guarantees, you need to learn a way of living from the center of yourself. Then you can map out your future career path from within that sturdy center. The new career paradigm must be time-based: How should you spend your time so as to best secure your future?

The evidence from futurists assures us that the breakneck speed driving our society will not slow down anytime soon. The mind-boggling pace of economic and political change in the world—from Europe and the Soviet Union to China and Japan—reminds us that America will keep running a hard race at least through this decade. Moreover, the uncertainty for workers will remain high. As hundreds of overleveraged corporations struggle to pay off debts, the usual quick fix will be to downsize the labor force. The global economy and global time are both here to stay.

Persistent signals from our society, especially the corporate culture, will ceaselessly urge you to HURRY, HURRY, HURRY, and will offer you in return not a single long-term promise. But you can steer your own course in this challenging era. You can set your own pace and succeed on your own terms. Here is the essence of the strategy I will show you: Get rid of the outmoded values that fueled American business over the past 30 years, and adopt instead a set of values honed to needs of the year 2000.

Forget the Career Ladder: It's Gone

Before you build a new career paradigm for the future, you must clear your head of the old ladder. The ladder depended for its viability on a trustworthy covenant honored by employer and employee alike, but we've seen that the covenant has been broken. Many corporations still use the metaphor of the career ladder: it serves the company's purpose in calling you to loyalties and commitments which enhance productivity. This ladder has no building against which you can lean it. Such a ladder, precariously balanced in midair, serves no useful purpose to you. Discard it.

Now you are ready to change your sense of identity within the corporate culture at large.

Seize Five Rings for the Future

Having discarded the image of the career ladder as a useful paradigm, you are ready to construct a new paradigm. Your future lies not at a given place but within yourself. You will work with other people within your present company but also beyond it through other companies. What you need are the kinds of skills and thinking/action patterns which will enable you to triumph in a fluid, ever-changing, fast-paced environment. What's more, you need special "helps" to compensate for the loss of security and camaraderie that buoy you up in a place where you are secure for the long term.

These helps, which I call the rings of power, together form a creative force to serve you—drawn from a rich and fertile past, with roots deep in both the Eastern and Western traditions. The term "five rings," in fact, comes from the classic book on martial strategy written by the Japanese Miyamoto Musashi in 1645. But the plan for action springs from the heart of the American frontier. These rings form a bold and effective amalgam of the traits that enabled pioneer men and women to forge a society out of a wilderness. Study these five rings of power. Make them your own. Use them to build your future successfully.

Visualize yourself in the center of a circle. This is where you stand in your career. You have analyzed your position and are doing everything possible to take back ownership of your time on the job. Now it is time to cast your eyes toward the future. Rimming the circle are five rings of power. You can call on them for strength and a sense of direction whenever you wish.

The First Ring: Self-Reliance

Instead of identifying yourself with a given corporation, think of yourself as a valuable person with a strong combination of skills to contribute. You can do an absolutely first-rate job for your company without sacrificing your independent spirit. If you stop restricting your horizons to your present company, you will get the time and energy to be self-reliant. Don't waste time identifying with your corporation in outmoded ways. Don't look to your boss as the key to your future. Look to yourself. Ask yourself: What do I have to offer and how can I make use of those skills, traits, accomplishments, and experience to strengthen my position?

In order to spend your time planning your future in realistic ways, you need to free yourself emotionally by creating a psychological distance between yourself and the corporation. That doesn't mean you perform any less competently. It's just that emotional energy takes up time, too. It stands to reason that if the old corporate pact is now an empty shell, and if companies are committed to a time-based organization which they recognize as the only way to compete in the upsurging global economy, then you have—in essence—only yourself to rely on.

But don't despair. This same thought has invigorated millions of people who flocked to these shores from the beginning—and still do—because self-reliance is the other side of a most precious coin: freedom. The quality of self-reliance, praised by Ralph Waldo Emerson, can serve you well. Look to yourself and thrive. Whether you construct a future plan which involves becoming an entrepreneur or not, you should adopt some of the entrepreneurial values: adventurousness, boldness, willingness to take risks. Although conventional business thinking sets the entrepreneurial type against the managerial or professional type, claiming that the two are opposite types, this need not be the case. These are new times, calling for a new mix of qualities to make for success. A generous dash of the entrepreneurial spirit is called for in the current corporate culture.

Take Time to Market Yourself

Stay on the team, but run your own race. Keep the timetable for your future fluid, but construct a strong, marketable image of yourself and circulate it both within and outside your company. When Drexel Burnham Lambert Inc., the leading purveyor of high-risk securities on Wall Street, suddenly filed for bankruptcy on February 13, 1990, and fired its 5,300 employees, most of them dumped the contents of their workstations into cardboard cartons and hit the streets in a state of panic and shock. Reemployment became a big problem for many, not only because they were in the worst possible condition psychologically to search for a job, but because they had to try to reenter an arena in which some 35,000 people had been fired since the stock market crash of 1987.

I talked to one of these Drexel Burnham executives who had made a fast transfer to a lucrative spot with a competing firm. "Did you foresee the collapse of Drexel several months ago," I asked, "and start looking for another post?"

"No, not at all," came the reply. "I was just as surprised as everybody else. It was an easy move for me because two other companies had been wooing me for two years. I took my pick between them."

Even though this executive had been working in a 12-hour-a-day, seven-day-a-week environment, when Michael Milken's junk bond deals were at their feverish peak, this executive took the time to market himself. He kept his skills and accomplishments continually visible on Wall Street. Most important, he hasn't stopped this process; it is necessary investment time in today's corporate culture.

Another executive I interviewed, now a bank president at a burgeoning organization, assessed his situation several years ago. As an economist teaching in a business college, he realized he had meager financial prospects and low visibility. But he did have financial expertise and credentials which were transferable to the banking industry. He started making himself visible. He took the time to create a marketing campaign, visiting bank executives on his own behalf. He got a top post at a savings and loan institution, but jumped off before that crashed. He has since moved twice, before becoming a bank president. Meanwhile, he secured his financial future. No longer dependent, he can truly work from a position of security achieved through self-reliance.

In marketing yourself, do it right. Sometimes we find it hard to get an objective view of ourselves. We can put forward a product, a service, a company, but not ourselves. It is not enough simply to prepare an updated résumé and try to take advantage, as we discussed in the last chapter, of everything your company offers in the way of further training. You need to spend time "packaging yourself" for the future. What direction do you want to grow and expand in? What work would you like to be doing five years from now? Think in terms of skills rather than companies. When you have created a marketing plan for yourself, then you need to present it carefully to other companies but possibly to your own company as well. A growing trend among companies is to ask headhunters to look over the in-house candidates.

Don't leave anything to chance. Spend the money to see a career counselor, a résumé writer, an image consultant, executive placement or testing firms. Make a video of yourself in action. Read books. Manage the packaging of yourself. Bring the same savvy intelligence to marketing yourself as you do to getting the work done for your company.

The Second Ring: Mutualism

You need to be self-reliant, and you need to face the fact that corporations don't offer the old-time security. But that doesn't mean you are alone. People matter more than ever. Mutualism is the strategy of seeking to build an active community of business friends. Look for areas of mutual competence, define places of mutual needs and goals. If you build up a relationship of mutual dependence and trust, then mutual help will naturally spring from that bond. The goal of mutualism is not a tit-for-tat relationship based on getting and giving favors—like a tipster on horse racing. Rather you seek ongoing, supportive relationships that transcend the particular workplace you're in at the moment and is based on your common situation, your professional commitment, and your long-range career goals. In a bond based on mutualism, both parties are dependent, both parties benefit, both parties are willing to contribute to the other's well-being and advancement.

Mutualism offers a way to build a new sense of community in an insecure environment. Mutualism helps you deal with uncertainty, ambiguity, fluidity. You create an emotional ambience in which people matter more than things. Just as a friend is much more than a contact, so too a community of business friends is more than a network. The old view of networking—you scratch my back and I'll scratch yours—is too narrow. It's an outmoded concept, inadequate for your current circumstances. Look for like-minded people both within and outside your company with whom you can form relationships that is rooted in your business and career interests, but not limited to them. You're looking for people who have similar values and goals, people whom you can trust, people who are worthy of your loyalty.

Get acquainted with people not in terms of their job titles or power status in a company, sizing up what they can do for you, but rather in terms of the personal and professional talents and values they have that you can learn from and benefit from in many ways. Loyalty crosses company lines. Shared competence and commitments transcend the usual corporate boundaries. The foundation of mutualism is integrity, candor, and trust.

Replacing Lost Mentors

The mentor system has been one of the saddest casualties of the delayering and restructuring of American corporations. Among the 3 to 4 million managers who lost out in the eighties were many mentors who paved the way for the youngest recruits to the corporate culture. But there are opportunities in the new structure, which has been described as a flattened pyramid. Out of the team-based structure will arise allegiance to knowledge and information rather than to owners, which was the chief orientation of the old-time manager. Peer mentoring can be a satisfying replacement. Sharing values with those you trust becomes more important than having a father or mother figure to ease the way ahead of you. Your orientation is to a shared enterprise.

Ann-Marie, the bank auditor whom you met in chapter two, came to me with a problem. In her previous position she had found a wonderful mentor in her boss. But she left that bank because she saw it was in a weak financial position and would probably be submerged in a takeover, which neither she nor her mentor, in Ann-Marie's judgment, would likely survive. In her new position, she confided to me, the competition among young auditors was fierce. How should she seek out mentors? Should she look only for older women? No, I said. In this climate look for like-minded people of both sexes and all ages. Make friends, not contacts, and expand your horizons beyond this bank.

Friendly Cells, Small Circles

Extend your circle of business friends beyond your present company. How do you recognize people worth trusting? If you like somebody you meet, that's a good start. Their values match yours. Build relationships, not a company personnel file. Put your faith in mutual respect, honest dealings, shared values, professional goals. Does it make you vulnerable to be candid about your goals and beliefs? Yes, it does. And you will be sure to make a few mistakes along the way. Does it put you at a disadvantage to be an honest person in a dishonest world? Only if it doesn't matter to you who you are. Integrity relates to spending the time of your life in a worthwhile manner.

Think of small intense circles which have potential for growing. Don't limit yourself to your own profession or field. Within your friendly cells of like-minded individuals, you may include doctors, lawyers, managers, executives, educators, artists, technicians, and politicians, as well as people from many other walks of life. You share mainly a mutual desire to expand the understanding and knowledge flowing between you rather than to set up barriers and restrictions.

The Third Ring: Playfulness

You can't be playful if you're exhausted from time pressure. You can't be playful if you're working 240 hours a month, as a recent survey by the American Bar Association showed 13 percent of lawyers are doing. But why should you be playful? Playfulness pertains to the imagination and the higher powers of the intelligence. It is out of a playful, spontaneous spirit that your best ideas often arise. It is out of relaxed, spur-of-the-minute brainstorming that your strongest prospects for the future may pop up before your mind's eye.

Researchers have long observed that playfulness and the qualities associated with it—spontaneity, experimentation, inquisitiveness, humor and laughter, leisureliness, openness, a kind of mental tinkering with ideas—produce the great bursts of creativity which are the mystery and glory of human genius. Thus you need to nourish and protect your playful spirit, or, if you've been terribly time-driven, resurrect it. It is a quality which operates both within yourself, when you are working alone, and when you work with others in the same spirit.

Marty, for example, the Californian you met earlier in this book, found tremendous exhilaration working at the peak of his creative energy with a venture group. It was only after a period of about one year, during which he put in consistently long hours, with as little as 4 or 5 hours of leisure per week, that his spontaneity began to fail him. He made a crash landing back to earth. His wife noticed his irritability and complained about it, but he was in too much of a fog from overextending himself to listen to her. Only when the project ended and Marty got a great deal of catching-up sleep did he find his playfulness and creativity bubbling back to the surface.

Numerous studies show, in fact, that people suffering from time urgency, as Marty was, deprive themselves not only of personal leisure time but also of sleep. Dr. David F. Dinges, a biological psychologist at the Institute of Pennsylvania Hospital in Philadelphia, said, "I can't think of a single study that hasn't found people getting less sleep than they ought to." Tests have demonstrated that chronic sleep loss impairs short-term memory as well as the ability to make decisions and concentrate; it also slows down reaction time. Eventually sleep deprivation destroys a person's capacity to feel pleasure or to laugh at a joke. Says Dr. Dinges: "By the fifth night, you've lost seven and a half hours, or virtually a whole night's sleep. That's the day when you're just praying to get through it."

Building Your Own Campfire

In the absence of stable corporations with long-term agendas and a body of committed employees, there is no longer a ready-made community where playfulness can naturally emerge. So you need to build your own synergetic circles, comforting campfires where you can feel free to be playful. As one top executive complained to me, "Nobody in today's business organization factors in thinking creatively as a necessary element. The whole emphasis is on action, on doing." Synergy adds up to more than the sum of its parts. It is that fantastic, exhilarating, creative energy which flows from a group of talented, like-minded people. Synergy bursts forth out of engaging others playfully in problem solving on a given project. In spending time constructing your career paradigm for the future, you need synergy as a replacement for the vanished paternalistic corporation of past decades. Band together whenever you can with other people to brainstorm around a campfire.

Creative Juices in the Ad Agency

Playfulness is useful in virtually every human endeavor. There's hardly an occupation that doesn't benefit from the flow of creative juices. But some of the greatest pressure to produce exciting ideas in a hurry occurs in the field of advertising. Today especially, advertising agencies are under the gun to originate brilliant campaigns that can spark the interest of a public long since saturated by commercials. A recent *New York Times* article discussed this problem, and reported that Edward H. Meyer, chairman and president of Grey Advertising in New York City, recently started a program called "Celebrating Creativity," to nourish and inspire his creative department.

The series included advertising executives and their clients. It began with a program presenting the Guarneri String Quartet, which focused on exploring the problems involved in creative teamwork. The second program featured Broadway actor Mandy Patinkin, who performed extemporaneously on a bare stage; he talked with the audience about taking risks and summoning up the courage to fail as part of the creative enterprise. One of the benefits of the program was to give Grey executives the courage to show clients their work in progress—something many in advertising are too scared to do because of the fear of failure.

"Keeping creative is extremely difficult," commented Jeffrey Wine, a creative supervisor at Grey. "I have to go to plays twice a week and see as many movies as I can to keep myself filled up with ideas."

The Fourth Ring: Knowledge

Knowledge is power, as Francis Bacon said in the sixteenth century. If we are time-pressured, it is partly because we haven't learned to use the new information technology to serve our purposes. We are driven by it, rather than driving it at our own pace. You need a new learning attitude for the hi-tech, high-speed environment of the corporate culture. Reverse the psychological atmosphere. Instead of being time driven by the computer clock (which is a race you can never win, anyway), put yourself in the driver's seat. Use the computer and telecommunications technology to serve your purposes. Be a driver of learning for yourself.

The computer has made it possible for us to get an almost infinite amount of data at the single stroke of a keyboard. But we can be inundated by data, overwhelmed beyond our capacity to cope. Data, if you don't know what to do with it and about it, can be a terrible burden. Data in itself has no value; it must be converted into useful information.

That is why you need to focus on data to realize that gathering data takes time and is therefore the first place where you should exercise your power of choice. What data should you gather? Should you be at the mercy of every document that lands on your desk? Do you have to answer every beep of every machine that signals it has data to present to you? Think about that, and remember that your time belongs to you. It is your decision to deal with data as you decide. In fact, it is more important to choose which facts not to gather than which facts to accumulate. The process of learning takes place as you sift out facts that don't serve your purpose. In today's information-glutted culture, everybody urges you to read everything. Resist! Data is not power; knowledge is.

But information is not knowledge, either. The conventional business advice suggests that raw data must be converted into information in order to serve a useful purpose. This doesn't go far enough. Information is merely interpreted data, and it is only as potentially useful as the interpretation. Information must be transformed into knowledge in order for it to have power for you. Working from a knowledge perspective means to ask yourself what you need to know and then to go after the data and information you need as a base for acquiring knowledge. If your time is truly precious, then decide not to squander it on absorbing information that goes above and beyond every useful purpose. Focus your time on attaining knowledge—the kind of knowledge that helps you accomplish projects and goals.

Technology can be both a means of knowledge and a source of knowledge. Make technology your servant, not your master. The emphasis should be on insight and synthesis, on working with colleagues and co-learners, on exploration, experimentation, and innovation.

Trusted Experts as a Source of Knowledge

Your workplace and your colleagues on the job can be good sources of knowledge, but they are not your only resources. Spend time thinking about what kind of knowledge you need and where you can best get it. Books, universities, and trusted experts in your field are all rich sources to be tapped. If you take time to eliminate all the sources of poor information that you generally expose yourself to—such as the office rumor mill, television shows, low-quality newspapers, and the like—you'll have plenty of time to explore better sources. While it is truer than ever that knowledge is power, there is not a scrap of validity in the old saw that "ignorance is bliss."

The Fifth Ring: The Empty Bag

The empty bag is a metaphor for a piece of equipment that is essential in a corporate culture marked by frantic speed, constant change, insecurity and uncertainty. It's a challenging environment in which to work, and you can certainly succeed in it, but I don't pretend to suggest that it is easy. The empty bag is what the Eastern tradition would call a void. It is an empty space within yourself. Think of it as a container for putting all the excess baggage that uses up your time wastefully.

Even when we focus very intensely on the time of our life, we tend to discount the paramount and obvious fact that emotions—the feelings that accompany us as we pass the hours of every day—take up time. Our emotions can either enrich us and enhance our hours, help us through the day, or they can burn us up, consume fuel that we need for positive purposes.

The empty bag is for you to deposit negative and wasteful emotions. Put into that bag angers, fears, insecurities, regrets, sorrows over the past, the accumulated frustrations and worries of the day. Refuse to allow negative energies to rob you of your precious time—whether they emanate from your own heart, or from emotions that other people dump on you. In the corporate culture today, you will inevitably encounter plenty of potentially harmful energy. Put it in your empty bag, and you will discover that this simple mental expedient can deliver enormous power to you. You now have a place for getting rid of frustrations, suspicions, worries, and insecurities that are the natural result of living in uncertain times with no guarantees.

Wayne's Use of the Five Rings of Power

Wayne, like so many others in corporate America, faces an insecure future. He still has his job at Sears, but has no idea how long that will last, and his retirement time is far in the future. Here is how Wayne, with Sharon beside him, has used the strategies of the five rings of power.

While Wayne was still in the grip of shock after surviving the Sears purge of 1989, Sharon, who had been a full-time homemaker, updated her computer skills and went back to work. They redistributed the child care and housekeeping chores to accommodate Sharon's new responsibilities; the children proved ready and able to share in those family tasks.

Wayne and Sharon both faced the fact that he belonged to a dying breed: the middle manager. He had no idea what transferable skills he had. First he made a sweep of all his contacts, discovering mainly a few dozen people in other companies who were in the same boat.

Then Wayne contacted a career counseling firm to have a professional assessment done and get a current professional résumé prepared. He felt the need of an outside objective view. The news was both good and bad. The bad news was that Wayne's skills were broad and general and of the very kind that were being eliminated in the ongoing delayering of middle managers: he clearly needed specialized skills. The good news was that his counselor identified several strong traits: he was a troubleshooter, a fast learner, demonstrated a positive attitude and a willingness to change.

But what direction should he take? What new skills should he acquire? Once again, Wayne decided to put out a call for help. He contacted his best friend from Sears, a systems engineer named Valerie, and asked her if she would like to form a small group of "brainstormers." In a jocular tone, he said, "You know the old Midwestern custom of all the neighbors getting together for a barn raising? How about if we get together and try to figure out how to build a future?"

Valerie agreed, and between the two of them they pulled in six others who were among the endangered species at Sears. They met initially two nights a week for wild, raucous talks that ranged all over the lot. Sometimes they shared hysterical laughter; at other times anger swirled around the room. There were tears too.

After a few meetings, a program evolved. They challenged one another to think up creative ideas, then they reacted and offered suggestions. It was as much an emotional support group as it was an information- and knowledge-building effort.

Valerie was the first to leave. The youngest member of the group and unencumbered, she felt free to join a venture group in which her engineering skills would play a vital role. She threw her savings in with three others and jumped in with both feet.

Wayne and Sharon, with a mortgage and two growing children, played it more cautiously. But within three months they had a plan. In the latest reorganization at Sears, Wayne had lost his secretary and had taken on computer work much more extensively than before. Fascinated, he perceived that the emerging corporate structure, devoid of middle managers but replete with computers, would need software specialists of a more sophisticated kind. While most companies brought in consultants from the outside for brief periods, Wayne speculated that software expertise plus intimate knowledge of daily productivity flow could be joined in a single position, yielding increased productivity and decreased cost.

To see if he had a viable idea, Wayne visited a nearby university and talked to the chairman of the computer science department. He was soon enrolled at night in a program called a second bachelor's degree: he takes only the advanced courses needed for a computer science major and will get another college degree for this shortcut effort. Within two years Wayne will have a highly marketable skill; he'll make a presentation showing the bottom-line costs to Sears, but if he isn't successful there, he is confident of landing another position in his suburb near Oak Brook, Illinois, home of many Fortune 500 companies.

Wayne and Sharon feel they've taken back the time of their lives. Their destiny is in their own hands. "Whatever happens with Sears," says Sharon, "we'll make it. The strain of all this hasn't affected our relationship. If anything, we've become closer."

And What about Melissa?

Melissa, the talented lawyer you met in the first chapter, won her junior partnership before her 30th birthday. Her immediate reactions were euphoric. She called dozens of people all over the country to share the good news, and took the rare step of spending a whole weekend with her lawyer-parents who were thrilled at her success.

Somehow, though, her plans to take a lengthy vacation didn't materialize. Before 10 days had passed, Melissa's schedule was as harried and hurried as ever. What kept her going for a while was the thrill of her new status, which eventually began to diminish as the deep layers of fatigue fought to surface.

When I contacted her after several months, wondering when, if ever, she would want to live a more time-integrated life, she gave me the news that she had met someone and gotten into a serious relationship. They were about to get married.

"He isn't somebody who lives to work," she told me. "His work ethic is that it's important but not the most important thing in his life."

Melissa admitted that they had already had some heated discussions about her work hours. "I suppose I will have to say no once in a while to bringing work home," she said. But her tone carried no conviction.

Melissa is at the very edge now, probably on the verge of being forced by her fiancé to begin making some hard choices. Perhaps the man she loves will serve as a catalyst for her discovery that a time-rich, time-integrated life is possible for her if she decides to reach out and take it.

Stop Worrying: Time Is on Your Side

In 1988, 29 percent of the workforce was aged 25 to 34 years, but by 2000, only 23 percent will be between 25 and 34. This means the youngest people entering the job market will be in a much stronger bargaining position. But regardless of your age, time is still on your side. The continuing computerization of the corporate culture, along with the fast-advancing pace of high technology across the whole society will require competent workers, and as workers smarten up, the pendulum will swing in your direction. Employers will face up to the fact that they ultimately will not be able to keep the stockholders happy if they can't keep the workforce satisfied.

You've developed a short-term as well as a long-range career plan. You've learned how to work in micro-time while thinking in macro-time. But don't engrave your plans in stone. The American corporate culture, as with the global marketplace, will continue its fast-paced, ever-changing way into the twenty-first century. Be ready to change and modify your goals as the situation warrants.

Keep educating yourself about the challenges, strategies, and skills needed for future business success. Rosabeth Moss Kanter, a professor at Harvard Business School, writes in her recent book, *When Giants Learn to Dance* (Simon & Schuster, 1989), "A formal title and its placement on the organization chart will have less to do with career prospects and career success than the skills and ideas a person brings to that work." Success will belong to those who know how to tap into their creative reserves.

Best Bets for the Future:

- SMALL BUSINESSES: Most business in the U.S. is small business. Nearly 80 percent of all U.S. businesses (excluding farms) employ fewer than 10 people. Of all nonfarm businesses here, 97 percent are considered small. The small business part of the economy creates more jobs than any other; it provides, directly or indirectly, the livelihood of more than 100 million Americans—that's almost half the current U.S. population. Cetron and Davies report in *American Renaissance* that small businesses—those with fewer than 100 workers, now employ nearly 60 percent of the workforce and are expected to generate half of all new jobs between now and the year 2000. In 1987, small businesses accounted for 1 million new jobs, compared to 97,000 from larger companies. By the year 2000, 85 percent of the labor force will be working for firms employing fewer than 200 people.
- WHAT ABOUT ENTREPRENEURS?: Some 1.2 million small firms have opened their doors over the past half-dozen years.

In 1989, about 200,000 entrepreneurs struck off on their own. According to Small Business Administration data, 24 of every 100 businesses starting out today are likely to have disappeared in two years, and 27 more will have closed up shop four years from now. But on the upside, a recent survey shows 77 percent of new businesses still thriving after three years. Most credited their success to having selected a business they already knew. Some 80 percent had worked with the same product or service in their previous jobs.

- NEW AND EMERGING OCCUPATIONS: Here is a useful, if obvious, secret. Those who successfully predict the future are those who understand the present most clearly. The future is contained in the present for those who have eyes to see. Opportunities will be for narrow specialists and top managers, while much of the actual work will be done by task-focused teams. Many new kinds of jobs will appear, and some of them may be just what appeals to you. Much information is available. The World Future Society puts out three periodicals: *The Futurist, World Future Society Bulletin,* and *Future Survey.* There's also *Occupational Outlook Quarterly, What's Next, National Business Employment Weekly,* and a host of other specialized resources which any reference librarian can bring to your attention.

Enjoying the Fullness of Global Time

In a global marketplace operating on global time, we now have the whole world at our doorstep, offering wonderful opportunities not even imagined 100 years ago. Every day 3 million people fly from one place on the planet to another. Authors John Naisbitt and Patricia Aburdene, in *Megatrends 2000,* point out that across the United States, 23,000 scheduled flights a day carried 450 million passengers in 1989. But by the year 2000 there will be 750 million. Today 1 billion passengers fly the world's airways each year. By the year 2000 it will be 2 billion passengers, *double* the 1990 figure.

Naisbitt and Aburdene speak of the emerging global lifestyle. "Lifestyle images speed around the globe at the velocity of light, diffusing their contents everywhere. Since fashion is faddish, speed is essential; if the information comes too late, you miss the fad." People everywhere are able to share food, fashion, entertainment, fun, film, magazines, television, and one another's company.

The Power Book

The little black book has assumed a transformed identity. There is a whole new class of young people coming of age today who are already at home in this new global time. I became acquainted with the story of a young man, traveling as a student, who had, in addition to the usual book of names and addresses, a small book he called his "book of forces." It contained the names of special people gifted in ways he admired. It was certainly not a list of possible job contacts. One person listed is a provocative thinker who is at work on an original theory of government. Others are artists or musicians. They include many different nationalities: a special family of people who care about the world and one another. This "book of forces" struck me as a symbol of the global lifestyle now possible in a richly personal way.

A Richer, Time-Integrated Life

There's a saying that has always appealed to me: Today is the first day of the rest of your life. Begin here, where you are, to live your life in a richer, more time-integrated way. It is not easy to rise above the pressure to run at the frantic pace that fuels our days. It is not simple to stop and take a deep breath, resolving to pace ourselves according to the deep rhythms that lie within our most private selves. But it *is* possible, and the struggle is worthwhile. At the top of the mountain, the view is stupendous.

AN ACTION PLAN FOR STAYING TIME-INTEGRATED

Now is the time to consolidate what you have learned from this book. To go forward confidently, you need to take steps to be sure that you will not lose any of the gains you have made. Here is the place to set in motion a maintenance plan for yourself. It is never enough to say that since you understand, everything will naturally happen for the best. In this last section let me show you how to stay a successful, time-integrated person.

Part I.   The Self-Nurturant Phase

1. Seek Out the Pleasures of Nature. Remember what Shakespeare wrote: "There's no clock in the forest." Go back to nature frequently to renew your awareness of internal rhythms with nature. Nature's time heals, refreshes, renews—combats the hurrying disease.
2. Exercise for Self-Discovery. Set up a regular program of enjoyable noncompetitive exercise. This is not to rule out competitive sports, but rather to be sure to include exercise which helps you to get in touch with the body's rhythms and to experience a feeling of belonging to yourself. You can go home to yourself, listen to your body's internal rhythms, through soothing, focused exercise. This is not to say you should avoid rigorous exercise. For some high-energy people, the need for strenuous effort is built into the genes. If your body has those kinds of exercise requirements, then go for it. The important thing is that the exercise you choose is satisfying in itself and not done according to somebody else's bodily rhythms, but yours alone. This exercise is to get in touch with your inner self through rhythmic movements of your body.
3. Reward Yourself with Personal Time. Promise yourself the reward of time for accomplishing a difficult task, for finishing a distasteful job, for no other purpose than pampering yourself. The important point is to convert into action the principle that you

need and deserve time for yourself alone. How lengthy the time modules are does not matter as much as how often you take these time rewards. Small fun times should become a taken-for-granted part of every day.

4. Pay Attention to Your Spiritual Self. Every person on earth has a spiritual dimension that needs to be nurtured in order to grow, develop, mature, and flourish. One of the greatest losses people suffer as a result of time distortion is the shrinking and withering of the spirit until it is reduced to nothing more than a small voice that occasionally screams, "help!" somewhere deep inside us. It is that part of you which expresses your sense of purpose and meaning in life. Meditation is the age-old route to the spiritual self. Choose the method that suits you best.

5. Pace Your Days to Your Own Inner Clock. Through following the above four steps, you will get in touch with the deepest rhythms of your unique self: that place where your sense of purpose, of dignity, of worthwhileness, resides. It is the spiritual center from which you have a deep need to live your life. From that still point within yourself flows the current of your life. You can hear yourself in time. From this point you can track the course of your days. Here resides the core of your personality. Here you find balance and harmony. To keep this inner clock ticking serenely, all you have to do is listen.

Part II.   The Friendship-Tending Phase

Through the centuries, the lessons of history and literature have shown us that—trite as it may sound—what matters most in life to people is other people. Time-harried men and women often unintentionally let the people they care about recede to a less and less significant corner of their lives. It's understandable. People in America are constantly moving, growing, changing, leaving—dropping out of one circle and joining another. You need to think of your friends and loved ones as moving across an ever-changing spectrum which requires your tending and attention. As some people move away, withdraw, fall out of the picture for one reason or another, you need to find others to replace them. Time spent with people we care about is what makes life most worthwhile in the long run. Remember that frequent, even if brief, contacts with others keeps us in touch. Don't make the mistake of believing that because you don't have a lot of time you can't keep up with friends—and I count relatives in the friendship category, too.

Part III.   The Corporate Watch Phase

The decade facing us is without doubt the most volatile and fast-changing in the history of humanity. The shifting sands of this global economy makes this dictum imperative: Stay alert to the changing corporate scene. Your career plan is not etched in stone. It must be as fluid as the times. Evaluate, update, and periodically alter your career plan. Do this task always with reference to the changing events in your corporate culture—which includes your company, your broader professional circle, and the economic environment at large. Don't rely on the company rumor mill. Don't waste time trying to get solid information from the TV set in your living room. Don't confine yourself to your local daily newspaper. Get the best sources of information for your career field, and tap into them regularly. Ordinarily these sources will be high-caliber newspapers, magazines, or journals, and trusted experts in your field. Identify those sources and go after them. The most time-consuming part of this task is to find the best information sources; keeping up with them will require less time than you probably give to TV network news right now.

Part IV.   Looking to the Global Future

The world is opening up, changing for the better. The quintessential American spirit has, from the beginning, been to look forward with an optimistic spirit. There is no reason to depart from that traditional outlook now. Quite the reverse. One of the best and most objective indicators is the "doomsday clock," which the top scientists of the world use as a rough indicator of the relative danger of all-out war. In 1990, these scientists pushed back the doomsday clock by 10 minutes. There are more opportunities than ever before to drink fully and deeply of the waters of our global civilization—to learn more, live more deeply, travel more extensively, know the peoples of this planet in a richer and more significant way. To become a time-integrated person, and to resolve to stay that way, is to open the door to enjoyment of those riches. In the new world that is upon us, we have become a globe of interdependent peoples with new opportunities for expanding the horizons of time. It is up to you and me, to all of us together.

Now, While You're Thinking of It . . .

Write your action plan for staying a time-integrated person. After each of the statements below, write as specifically as you can exactly HOW you will put into practice that step. Answer both in MACRO time and MICRO time.

Part I. NURTURING MYSELF

1. I will seek out the pleasures of nature:

. . . .

. . . .

. . . .

2. I will exercise for self-discovery:

. . . .

. . . .

. . . .

3. I will reward myself with personal time:

. . . .

. . . .

. . . .

. . . .

4. I will pay attention to my spiritual self:

. . . .

. . . .

. . . .

. . . .

5. I will pace my days to my own inner clock:

. . . .

. . . .

. . . .

. . . .

Part II. TENDING MY FRIENDSHIPS

1. Name 3 or 4 friends who live in another city:

. . . .

. . . .

. . . .

. . . .

. . . .

I will get in touch with them in the following ways, and, if it is
possible to see them in person, indicate how and when:

. . . .

. . . .

. . . .

. . . .

2. Name 2 friends who live in your own city whom you haven't been in
touch with for 6 months:

. . . .

. . . .

Here is what I will do to reconnect with these two friends:

. . . .

. . . .

. . . .

3. Name 1 business acquaintance you have met recently who seemed
likable and interesting:

. . . .

I will schedule a lunch with this person within the next two weeks

. . . .

. . . .

. . . .

Part III.   THE CORPORATE WATCH PHASE

I have identified the following reading materials as probable sources of
good information in my field. After each publication, I will list my
specific intention to read them:

. . . .

. . . .

. . . .

. . . .

I recognize the following people as accessible experts in my field. I will
make an effort to get together with them within the next two weeks:

. . . .

. . . .

Part IV.   THE GLOBAL FUTURE

The world is full of wonderful opportunities to make life more
pleasurable and exciting. Keeping in mind that I pass through this
life just once, here is my wish list of dreams that I will pursue in
the coming year: (Don't be constrained by narrow realism here.
Dream a great dream!)

. . . .

. . . .

. . . .

. . . .

. . . .

. . . .

AFTERWORD . . . CHECK UP ON YOURSELF

Mark the following dates, counting from today:

1 month   . . . .

3 months   . . . .

6 months   . . . .

12 months   . . . .

On the dates marked above, review your answers and rewrite your action plan in accordance with the passing time. Now please enjoy the time of your life!

BIBLIOGRAPHY

Bennett, Amanda. *The Death of the Organization Man.* New York: William Morrow and Co., 1990.

Berman, Phyllis W. and Frank A. Pedersen, eds. *Men's Transitions to Parenthood: Longitudinal Studies of Early Family Experience.* Hillsdale, New Jersey: Erlbaum, 1986.

Block, Peter. *The Empowered Manager: Positive Political Skills at Work.* San Francisco: Jossey-Bass, 1987.

Boslaugh, John. "The Enigma of Time." *National Geographic.* March, 1990.

Cetron, Marvin and Owen Davies. *American Renaissance: Our Life at the Turn of the 21st Century.* New York: St. Martin's Press, 1989.

Csikszentmihalyi, Mihaly. *Flow: The Psychology of Optimal Experience.* New York: Harper & Row, 1990.

Deutsch, Claudia H. "When a Handshake Isn't Enough." *New York Times,* February 4, 1990.

Egan, Timothy. "A Stroll in the Country for City Dwellers, Starting Downtown." *The New York Times.* June 24, 1990.

Foltz, Kim. "Grey Series Urges Risks for Creativity." *New York Times,* May 1990.

Fraser, J.T., N. Lawrence, and F.C. Haber, eds. *Time, Science, and Society in China and the West: The Study of Time.* Volume V. Amherst: The University of Massachusetts Press, 1986.

Friedman, Meyer and Ray H. Rosenman. *Type A Behavior and Your Heart.* New York: Knopf, 1974.

Gendlin, Eugene. *Focusing.* New York: Everest House, 1978.

Goodman, Ellen. "Blessed Be The Ties That Bind?" *The Gainesville Sun.* July 22, 1990.

Grove, Noel. "Greenways: Paths to the Future." *National Geographic.* June 1990.

Hall, Edward T. *The Dance of Life: The Other Dimension of Time.* New York: Anchor, 1984.

Hochschild, Arlie. *The Second Shift: Working Parents and the Revolution at Home.* New York: Viking Penguin, 1989.

Jacobson, Gary and John Hillkink. *Xerox: The American Samurai.* New York: Macmillan, 1986.

Kanter, Rosabeth. *When Giants Learn to Dance.* New York: Simon & Schuster, 1989.

Kiechel, Walter, III. *Office Hours: A Guide to the Managerial Life.* Boston: Little, Brown & Co., 1988.

Kilborn, Peter T. "Work, Work, Work!" *Tampa Tribune.* June 10, 1990.

Lakein, Alan. *How To Get Control of Your Time and Your Life.* New York: NAL, Signet, 1973.

Lamb, Michael E., ed. *Nontraditional Families: Parenting and Child Development.* Hillsdale, New Jersey: Erlbaum, 1982.

Lamb, Michael E., ed. *The Father's Role: Applied Perspectives.* New York: Wiley-Interscience, 1986.

Landes, David S. *Revolution in Time: Clocks and the Making of the Modern World.* Cambridge: Harvard, 1983.

Levinson, Jay Conrad. "Accessing Your Unconscious to Gain More Time." *The Ninety-Minute Hour: Technological and Psychological Breakthroughs Take You Beyond Time Management.* New York: E. P. Dutton, 1990.

Mackenzie, Alec. *The Time Trap: The New Version of the Classic Book on Time Management.* New York: American Management Association, 1990.

Mackay, Harvey. *Swim With the Sharks Without Being Eaten Alive.* New York: William Morrow & Co., 1988.

Mayer, Jeffrey, J. *If You Haven't Got the Time to Do It Right, When Will You Find the Time to Do It Over? The Time Management System That Will Save You Up to an Hour a Day.* New York: Simon & Schuster, 1990.

Monk, Pamela. "Canoe Camping, Family Style." *The New York Times.* June 24, 1990.

Moskowitz, Robert. *How To Organize Your Work And Your Life: Proven Time Management Techniques for Business, Professional, and Other Busy People.* New York: Doubleday, 1990.

Murray, Thomas J. "Managing for the Global Decade." *Business Month,* July 1989.

Musashi, Miyamoto. *A Book of Five Rings: The Classic Guide to Strategy.* Translated by Victor Harris. Woodstock, New York: The Overlook Press, 1974.

Naisbitt, John and Patricia Aburdene. *Megatrends 2000: Ten New Directions for the 1990's.* New York: William Morrow and Co., 1990.

Omsted, Barney and Suzanne Smith. *Creating A Flexible Workplace: How To Select and Manage Alternative Work Options.* New York: Amacon, 1989.

Pascale, Richard Tanner. *Managing On The Edge: How The Smartest Companies Use Conflict To Stay Ahead.* New York: Simon & Schuster, 1990.

Peters, Thomas J. and Robert H. Waterman, Jr. *In Search of Excellence: Lessons From America's Best-Run Companies.* New York: Warner Books, 1982.

Peters, Thomas J. *Thriving on Chaos: Handbook for a Management Revolution.* New York: Knopf, 1987.

Pierpont, Margaret. "Future Fitness? Mind Health." *Self,* March 1989.

Rifkin, Jeremy. *Time Wars.* New York: Henry Holt, 1987.

Rimer, Sara. "Fitness and Solitude." *The New York Times.* April 29, 1990.

Roediger, David R. and Philip S. Foner. *Our Own Time: A History of American Labor and the Working Day.* Westport, Connecticut: Greenwood Press, 1990.

Rose, Kenneth Jon. *The Body in Time.* New York: John Wiley & Sons, Inc., 1988.

Schlenger, Sunny and Roberts Roesch. *How to Be Organized in Spite of Yourself: Time & Space Management That Works with Your Personal Style.* New York: NAL, 1989.

Shaevitz, Marjorie H. *The Superwoman Syndrome.* New York: Warner Publications, 1984.

Stalk, George, Jr. and Thomas M. Hout. *Competing Against Time: How Time-Based Competition Is Reshaping Global Markets.* New York: The Free Press, 1990.

Thurow, Lester. *The Zero-Sum Solution.* New York: Simon & Schuster, 1986.

Zuboff, Shoshana. *In the Age of the Smart Machine: The Future of Work and Power.* New York: Basic Books, 1988.